TEACHING, LEARNING, AND THE MEDITATIVE MIND

J. Richard Wingerter

University Press of America,® Inc.
Lanham · New York · Oxford

Copyright © 2003 by
University Press of America,® Inc.
4501 Forbes Boulevard
Suite 200
Lanham, Maryland 20706
UPA Acquisitions Department (301) 459-3366

PO Box 317
Oxford
OX2 9RU, UK

ISBN 0-7618-2548-7 (clothbound : alk. ppr.)
ISBN 0-7618-2549-5 (paperback : alk. ppr.)

∞™ The paper used in this publication meets the minimum
requirements of American National Standard for Information
Sciences—Permanence of Paper for Printed Library Materials,
ANSI Z39.48—1984

Contents

Acknowledgments

For advice and for reading and commenting on the initial draft of this work, the author expresses thanks to Dr. Evelina M. Orteza y Miranda of the University of Calgary and R.E. Mark Lee of the Krishnamurti Foundation of America. Thanks is also expressed to Linda Lentz for preparation of the final copy for printing.

The author is most grateful and expresses thanks to the Krishnamurti Foundation of America, Ojai, California, Krishnamurti Foundation Trust Limited, Brockwood Park, Bramdean, Hampshire, U.K., and Mirananda, The Hague, Netherlands, for permission to reprint material from J. Krishnamurti, *A Flame of Learning*: *Krishnamurti with Teachers* (The Hague: Mirananda, 1993). Copyright 1993 Krishnamurti Foundation Trust Limited. Reprinted with the permission of the Krishnamurti Foundation of America, Ojai, California.

Knowledge can be taught, but not wisdom ....
Knowledge is not the coin for the purchase of wisdom.

To understand life is to understand ourselves, and that is both the beginning and the end of education.

Education may mean opening the doors of perception to the vast movement of life. It may mean learning how to live happily, freely, not with hate and confusion, but in beatitude.

Self-knowledge is the beginning of wisdom; without self-knowledge, learning leads to ignorance, strife, and sorrow.

J. Krishnamurti

Introduction

A Call for Revolution in Education

It is very often said that there is need for change in education. Most, if not all, calls for such change are not radical for they are merely calls for change relative to the superficial, to partial functioning of the mind and not at all to what has great depth, namely, the truly meditative mind. This book might be said to be a call for revolution in education such that there be concern on the part of teachers and students for meditative mind awareness and for what such awareness makes possible, that there be cultivation in schools and universities of not just proper partial mind functioning but also, significantly, cultivation by teachers and students of the truly meditative mind.

This is the third book by this author, and in this book, as in the other two,[1] there is a description or expression of the action of negation out of a "meditatorlessly" meditative mind. In the first book the expression and negation had to do with observerless observation of things said and written in philosophy, and in the second, with things said and written in relation to science and religion. In this book they have to do with education. The negation which is described in chapters one and three of this volume is intended to show the inadequacies, indeed the falseness of things said by writers in education relative to their calls for educational change. Such negation is there whenever there is seeing "the false as false," and such seeing always "is in itself enough, for that very perception frees the mind from the false."[2] To put this point somewhat differently, one can say, as Krishnamurti himself said, that "to see the truth in the false is the beginning of wisdom; to see the false as the false is the highest comprehension .... Only by understanding the false as the false is there freedom from it."[3] Krishnamurti also said that "negative thinking is the highest form of intelligence," and that "to see the false as the false ... mind must be capable of direct perception; if it is not, it will be lost in the jungle of ideas, opinions, and beliefs."[4] Yet again there is expressed wisdom in Krishnamurti's words: "When the false has dropped away, there is freedom for that which is not false to come into being. You cannot seek the true through the false; the false is not a stepping-stone to the true. The false must cease wholly."[5] Once there is the understanding which comes of meditative mind negation, of its choiceless, observerless seeing of the false as the false, then there can be the profound, revolutionary change which is described and called for, particularly in the second and last chapters of this book, rather than any so-called change which is mere modification of what is or of what has been. Indeed, as Krishnamurti said, "any revolution" merely "within the field of time, the field of the known ... is no revolution at all, but only a modification of what has been."[6]

When there is commentary below by the author, called the commentator, relative to statements made by Krishnamurti, it might be said that the mind of the author is on the same level as was that of Krishnamurti when he spoke the statements quoted, that in the case of the author there is the same concern, the same intensity which were always those of Krishnamurti. If this is indeed the case, then it seems right to say that what is written in the commentary parts of this book is consonant with the thinking of Krishnamurti as this is expressed in his writings. Whether or not this is really and always, or most often, the case is for readers, or at least those readers who have read Krishnamurti extensively, to judge, or rather to see, observerlessly, choicelessly.

Chapter One

Teaching, Learning, and the Partially Functioning Mind

> Our present education ... teaches us to love success and not what we are doing. The result has become more important than the action.

> Education is not merely acquiring knowledge, gathering and correlating facts; it is to see the significance of life as a whole.

J. Krishnamurti

There are many inadequacies, indeed much falseness in a great deal of what is written today relative to education and calls for change to it. While the commentary in this first chapter points to the essential need for the cultivation of properly partially functioning minds in schools and universities, it also points out inadequacies and falseness in what is said by John P. Miller, J.R. Bruce Cassie, and Susan M. Drake in *Holistic Learning: A Teacher's Guide to Integrated Studies*,[1] Stuart Parker in *Reflective Teaching in the Postmodern World: A Manifesto for Education in Postmodernity*,[2] and Tobin Hart in *From Information to Transformation: Education for the Evolution of Consciousness*.[3] All of these serve as examples of the numerous books in the area of education which contain the same or similar inadequacies or falsehoods. When there is seeing of the inadequacies and falseness in these books, there comes to mind the realization that there is need, in education, for profound change or transformation, possible when there is a valuing of the truly meditative mind, an awakening of the mind to the importance or significance of meditative mind awareness. We begin with an examination of things said by Miller, Cassie, and Drake.

1.0

Miller, Cassie, & Drake: The holistic curriculum attempts to restore a balance between linear thinking and intuition ... metaphor and visualization can be integrated with more traditional thinking approaches so that a synthesis is achieved.

Commentator: Any so-called holism resulting from a combining of two aspects or parts of a partially functioning mind, from synthesizing right and left hemisphere functioning of the brain, could not be anything other than a mere fashioning by a partially functioning mind and, contrary to what is so often suggested today, cannot at all relate to a full, deep understanding of life, cannot at all be an appropriate answer to questions about living, to problems as regards right relationship with others, or with the world. It is illusion to think that any such approach as this will lead to living in relationship to wholeness, to fullness of living.

1.1

Miller, Cassie, & Drake: Ultimately, the holistic curriculum lets us connect with the deepest part of ourselves ... through the arts ... through mythologies which deal with the universal concerns of human beings.

Commentator: If the "deepest part of ourselves" in this statement means inner self, soul, or Atman, as it indeed seems to, then it relates to illusion, to falsehood, and it does not, indeed cannot, have anything to do with what is really, actually universal, namely, life, the living, what *is*. It has to do only with what is imagined, merely mind-created, what someone might say should be a reality but actually is not. Also, this statement has nothing to do with what is profoundly human but merely with what is projected out of a partially functioning mind and called human.

The arts are important, but they cannot be a way of capturing what is living, the eternal, the mystery which is the unknown. They, as much as left-brain fashionings, like ideas, concepts, and theories, have to do with mere creations of a partially functioning mind, mind functioning, that is, in relationship to time, experience, the known. Mythologies are always mere creations of a partially functioning mind and have nothing at all to do with living truth. As such they cannot speak to fundamental questions about right living, right relating.

1.2

Miller, Cassie, & Drake: Human processes involve activities that allow humans to make sense and meaning out of life. [One] way of making sense in a transactional and transformational way is through the use of *metaphor* ... metaphor can facilitate integrated learning. [One level] of metaphoric teaching ... is the *inventive*, through which the metaphor leads the individual to a new level of awareness and creative perception.

Commentator: Deep meaning in life is not something which is made or fashioned by a partially functioning mind. Rather, it comes to or is discovered in the state of the truly meditative mind. The action which is love, the only real action there is, requisite to one's really understanding the meaning of life, of living, is not at all a mere activity in which a partially functioning mind engages itself. Mere right brain fashionings of a partially functioning mind, that is symbols and metaphors, no more than a left brain partially functioning mind with its ideas and concepts can lend support or lead to integrated learning. Not even the results of an attempt to amalgamate or synthesize what each type of partial functioning produces can make for the integration which is possible in the state of the truly meditative mind.

One can say that intuition and invention have a place in relationship to the physical aspects of living, to the creation of scientific theories which can lead to the advancement of science and ease of living in time, as Einstein suggested in his famous statement about intuition being more important than knowledge, but there is no place for imagination and invention as regards matters psychological, as regards living and relating rightly. What so-called inventive metaphoric teaching can lead to is not new awareness and really creative perception. As an activity of the partially functioning mind, indeed functioning inappropriately when the matter is living, it necessarily has to do with what is old and dead. Truly creative perception is observerless, choiceless perception out of a truly meditative mind and not that perception which entails observer observing, choosing.

1.3

Miller, Cassie, & Drake: Educators can turn to the wisdom contained in the ancient mythologies for a framework for living for young people.

Commentator: Any such so-called wisdom is not real wisdom, wisdom which is there in the state of the truly meditative mind. Mythologies, ancient or newly-fashioned, with their images and symbols supposedly better related to living than the ideas and concepts fashioned by a left-brain, rationally functioning mind, are themselves mere fashionings of a partially functioning mind, of a mind functioning inappropriately when it deals in imagination and speculation as a way to understanding something about what *is*.

Experience has nothing at all to do with what is living, the eternal, the unknowable but rather is always related to the past, the known, the merely temporal. Rather than merely focusing on so-called "lived experience" as a right-brain functioning mind might attempt to do, there can be a totally silent mind experiencing the living, moment to moment, day to day, that which a partially functioning mind can quickly turn into experience. When a merely partially functioning mind attempts to deal with experience, appropriately as in science and in relationship to matters technological but inappropriately as regards matters psychological, it is focused on what is old and dead and not what is living, new, dynamic. Since mythologies are in the house of the dead, how could they possibly provide a framework for living for anyone? When there is the truly meditative mind, there can be real fullness of living. When there is not, one lives in a box, a framework, a structure created by a partially, rationally or irrationally functioning mind.

1.4

Miller, Cassie, & Drake: Campbell believes that educators today are in a position to begin creating a new myth with students. This is a myth of the planet; a myth that speaks to the interdependence among all things and emphasizes caring, compassion, peace, and harmony, [that] will ... guide education, shape our emotional attitudes, energize our actions, and provide us with life's purpose.

Commentator: Engagement in processes to create any myth is dealing in imagination. Once the myth is fashioned, what was and is imagined is talked about as that which ought, could, might, should be. It does not at all relate to reality, to what *is*. Any educator who would seek to do what Campbell is said here to believe is important would be engaged in effort to lead students "down the garden path," so to speak, that is, into illusion. Imagination, as regards living or relating, creates illusion. It is illusion also which would cause one to think that a merely partially functioning mind, specifically a right-brain partially functioning one, can lead to real caring, compassion, peace, and harmony. All it can do is project out of itself images and symbols of such things, or in the case of left-brain partial functioning, ideas and concepts of them. Real compassion and peace can come to the mind only when it is in a meditative state. It is likewise profound illusion to think that a partially functioning mind or anything which it creates can give people real meaning and purpose in living.

1.5

Miller, Cassie, & Drake: The inner journey or growth toward wholeness [is] the path of personal growth .... The reward of the journey can be no less than a transformation of consciousness .... The last stage is to completely sacrifice the old consciousness and return to the world in a new state of consciousness. It then becomes the duty of the journeyer to share new-found knowledge with the society in which she or he lives.

Commentator: One who is on any so-called "inner journey or growth toward wholeness" walks or treads along a path to illusion. One who arrives at the end of such a journey, or at some milestone along the way, can easily make the kind of exaggerated, extravagant claims we read about in this statement. All consciousness is old. When there is any so-called "transformation of consciousness," any so-called "new state of consciousness," such does not at all relate to that real revolution of the mind which gives the complete understanding and depth of insight which are vouchsafed only to the truly meditative mind. Furthermore, what "the journeyer" might share once he has arrived at any so-called enlightenment which supposedly comes at the end of the journey is the sharing of illusion and ignorance. What there is in the end, if and when the sharing talked about here is what a teacher does with students in a classroom, is undue conditioning of the minds of students, or at least effort unduly to condition such minds. If the conditioning of such minds is actually effected by the teacher, then what we have in this case is one who is blind leading the blind.

1.6

Miller, Cassie, & Drake: The journey of awareness involves a winding path along which one proceeds toward wisdom and wholeness.

Commentator: Whether such a path is straight or winding, it leads, inevitably, not to wisdom and wholeness but rather to ignorance and illusion. That all awareness is not consciousness is not an understanding that is reflected in this statement. Only when awareness as consciousness is ended in the state of a truly meditative mind can there be real wisdom, real wholeness. Only when time and all that is time-related are ended is there the living, the eternal, that which alone relates to deep insight, understanding, intelligence, and order in living.

1.7

Miller, Cassie, & Drake: Characteristically the journey involves a death of the world as it has been known, a struggle to reach the threshold of something new, and a rebirth [or] a return to the world with a new identity.

Commentator: If there is merely death to one partially functioning mind created system or structure and its replacement by another similarly created system or structure, merely struggle to move from one point in the whole of consciousness to another, or to recapture or return to an earlier point within the whole of consciousness, this cannot relate to anything new. The eternally new and living unlimited can be there only when the old, the temporal, the dead, the limited ceases. To replace one so-called identity with another, one which fundamentally is no different from the original one because it also is merely partially functioning mind created, is mere movement within the limits of experience, the known, the old, the dead and gone and not at all to the new, dynamic, ever-changing. For a teacher or educator to condition the minds of students in accord with what is suggested in this statement is to promote illusion and ignorance.

1.8

Miller, Cassie, & Drake: Stories in mythology have been passed down through the ages because they speak to the hearts and reveal the inner voice of generation after generation.

Commentator: Mythology relates not to what *is* but rather merely to what is imagined, wished for, yearned for. The implication in this statement is that myths contain wisdom. The hearts and inner voice spoken of here have to do with some illusory creation of a partially functioning mind, perhaps a believed in soul, Atman. For a teacher to revel in mythological stories or to think that these contain profound wisdom, and for her or him to suggest to students in a classroom that these deal with living truth is for this teacher to be in illusion and for him or her to attempt to lead students down a path to illusion, to ignorance.

1.9

Miller, Cassie, & Drake: Another human theme that could be explored is that of conflict. Mythology tells us that conflict is often experienced as tension between two existing opposites or dualities. Examination of this conflict illustrates that both of the opposites are necessary for the conflict to exist at all.

Commentator: Though conflict can indeed be seen as "tension between two ... opposites or dualities," opposites or dualities, as far as living or relating is concerned, are not real but merely fashionings by a partially functioning mind, as are the stories or myths which are believed, particularly by some of those who prize right rather than left-brain functioning, to contain profound wisdom and able therefore to suggest good guidelines for living. It is folly for teachers themselves to continue going down and leading others down a path to illusion, as they are doing when they themselves believe and condition the minds of students to believe that there is value in myths relative to the understanding of right living.

When opposites or dualities are there in relation to matters psychological, to living-truth matters, these are merely partially functioning mind created, unlike those opposites which are real because they are on the level of the physical. Real opposites are ones like day and night, man and woman. Opposites which are merely partially functioning mind created are transcended or gone beyond when there is mind in a truly meditative, fully understanding state.

1.10

Miller, Cassie, & Drake: It is possible to relate to the world within the framework of ... three positions (transmission, transaction, and transformation). At the transmission level there can be a tendency to see the world as an object to be manipulated .... At the transaction level we tend to relate to the world through our mental processes .... At the transformation level we relate to the world through our Being ... which allows us to see the world as interdependent and interconnected. Human processes at this level are characterized by a sense of discovery and wonder.

Commentator: The possibility and the relating spoken about here are totally related to a merely partially functioning mind. Thus the transformation also spoken about does not relate to that radical, profound change which has to do with awareness of the importance or the significance of not just conscious awareness but awareness on the level of the meditative mind.

The Being spoken about here is merely a mental construct fashioned by a partially functioning mind. It is merely an abstract vision of wholeness, something unreal, an image or a concept, perhaps something merely wished for, something imagined that is there when there is talk of an "interdependent and connected" world and not that whole which is the living, that with which the truly meditative mind communes. Of what value is wonder on the part of a self relating to what is unreal, that is, Being, a world merely envisioned? Anything which such a self discovers can only be some projection out of itself which is as unreal, as illusory as this Being, this world. For a teacher to indulge in what this statement implies and to attempt to have students do the same is for this teacher to deal in what is illusory, what is false. It is not anything related to wisdom, but rather to mere folly.

1.11

Parker: [There can be a] shift away from the realist conventions of academia to the literary play of postmodernism.

Commentator: What is talked about here is merely a shift from emphasis on left to right-brain partial mind functioning. The result as regards living or relating can only be one's dealing in the fragmentary, all the while indulging the self or Self which is wrongly believed to be something ultimately real, even one's supposing that then deeply significant things are being said and done. What is often the result of a prizing of right over left-brain partial mind functioning is an undervaluing of the proper role of rationality, of the strictness, but limited correctness, of objective thinking, as in science, a turning away from strict rationality so as to create right-brain related illusions.

1.12

Parker: Reflective teaching is centrally concerned with emancipation through enlightenment, through the activity of securing improvement in rationality ... and in ethics.

Commentator: What is important to ask when this kind of statement is heard or read is: What is real freedom? What is real enlightenment? Given an understanding of the possibility of awareness which is not consciousness and of a meditative and not just a rationally or intuitively functioning mind, as well as the understanding that real freedom and enlightenment are there only when there is awareness which is not consciousness, when there is the truly meditative mind, then there is also the understanding of the inadequacy of the suggestion made here. A simple attempt to improve rationality and any ethics related to it, and this by greater emphasis on right-brain partial mind functioning, cannot lead to full freedom of the mind, to total enlightenment of the mind, hence to complete, radical transformation of the mind. All of these considerations have important implications for teaching and learning. Much more than is now thought possible in educational settings is possible when there is understanding that besides time there is eternity, besides awareness which is conscious awareness there is awareness which is not conscious awareness, and besides a partially functioning mind there can be a truly meditative mind.

1.13

Parker: The tyranny of technical-rationalism ... and its austere view of the precinct of reason, is the predominant tradition against which reflective teachers seeking enlightenment and emancipation must struggle.

Commentator: Reflection is as limited as reasoning. Neither one of these, nor any joining or synthesis of the two partially functioning mind activities which these are, can lead to real freedom and enlightenment of the mind. Apart from the question as to whether or not right-brain related intuition has any other value than the one which relates to the part it plays in the arts and in the development, for example, of new scientific theories is the question of what is beyond all left and right-brain partial mind functioning.

1.14

Parker: Reflective teaching holds the self to have a real nature which, in its fundamental constitution, is rational.

Commentator: The self, rational or otherwise, is not anything ultimately real or actual. It is illusion to think that it is, and to base what is done in educational settings on such illusion is to be confused and in error, to be engaged in keeping students in or leading them into confusion and error. There is the rational mind, but it is limited. To understand its limits and thus to employ it appropriately, but also to stop rational mind functioning when such stopping is appropriate, is to have a mind related to what *is* and never to what is unreal, to what is illusion.

1.15

Parker: Truth is a product of the stories we tell ... there will be as many truths as there are stories.

Commentator: This suggests that truth is related to right-brain rather than left-brain functioning. Living truth, however, is not at all related to a partially functioning mind, be that functioning left or right-brain related. Living truth is absolute because related to what *is*, and not at all the relative thing spoken about here which is merely something created on the level of a partially functioning mind. If all students ever do in a classroom or outside of it is tell stories, and listen to the stories their teachers and others tell them, they are ever in the house of the dead.

1.16

Parker: The world speaks our language, fits our criteria ... truth coincides with our decisions ... the world coincides with how we take it to be.

Commentator: This is subjectivism versus objectivism, or idealism versus realism. That truth is relative is also the suggestion being made here. Beyond all opposites, including subject versus object and vice versa, and beyond any characterization of and claims made with regard to partially functioning mind fashioned truth is what *is*, living truth, that with which the truly quiet mind communes.

1.17

Parker: The questions of ... distortion versus clarity, illusion versus truth ... no longer seem to be interesting or useful questions to ask *in general* outside of the consideration of one particular case or another. [In this respect they are] like questions such as 'What is beauty?' ... or 'What is the nature of goodness?'

Commentator: This statement, made out of a partially functioning mind, reflects a failure to realize the value of a truly meditative mind. In the state of the truly meditative mind fundamental questions related to what truth, beauty, and goodness *really* are not only can be asked but indeed can be answered. Were a teacher or an educator never to "go into" such questions with students, he or she, so to speak, would be shortchanging them.

1.18

Parker: The   teacher-deconstructor   is   the   postmodern educationalist.

Commentator: Deconstruction on the part of someone whose mind only and always functions partially is not the same as negation out of a truly meditative mind. Whether one is right or wrong to say that deconstruction is the way to bring about clarity and proper thinking on the level of a partially functioning mind, and so teachers either do or do not have a responsibility to be deconstructors, can it not be said that teachers have a responsibility themselves to value the truly meditative mind and to communicate with students as regards the importance of meditative mind awareness? It is understandable that a teacher or educator would say that his or hers is indeed such a responsibility when hers or his is an understanding of the real dualism of time and the timeless, of the possibility of awareness which is not consciousness, and of the importance of communion of a truly meditative mind with the living.

1.19

Parker: [As a result of postmodern education] students and teachers ... will recognize that each position, each commitment or belief is contingent: its foundations are epiphenomena of its narrative; its truths are symbols which conceal a politics and an ethics.

Commentator: It might be said that contingency does indeed apply to all partially functioning mind related positions, commitments, and beliefs. Politics and ethics, moreover, are fundamentally symbols, fashionings made by a partially functioning mind. Having said all of this, however, one can then go on to say that there can be awareness of a different, deeper level of the mind, so to speak, a level of mind on which there are not, and cannot be positions, commitments, and beliefs. There can be, this is to say, a stopping of partial mind functioning, a negation of any and all fashionings of a partially functioning mind such that there can then be that full functioning of the mind which makes possible discovery of the absolute and understanding of living truth. Surely, if all of this is possible, then teachers must at some point and in some way work with students so that there can be fullness of understanding, and deep, loving intelligence related to the way they live their lives.

1.20
Parker: Postmodernists probe the limits of persuasion, testing what might prove to be dirty tricks on an audience to see if through winning they can earn the honorific title: *rational*. No general principle inhibits this 'anything goes' abandon.

Commentator: What the speaker or writer of a statement like this is promoting is what he or she might say is better functioning of the rational mind. All of the mind, however, is not merely partially functioning for there can also be, besides such functioning, absolute, total silence of the mind. Though with regard to the truly silent mind there is no place for "persuasion," "dirty tricks," "winning" and losing, and "honorific" titles, such a mind is of inestimable, immeasurable worth. Should not education involve concern, not only for proper partial mind functioning, whatever this is determined rightly to be, but also and significantly for meditative mind awareness?

1.21
Parker: Postmodern learning [can] equip students and teachers with a repertoire of rhetorical manoeuvres and literary devices; the weapons with which they can be empowered to fight the battle for change, and the achievement of an identity, in the postmodern revolution.

Commentator: Any change resulting from the activity spoken about here would not be profound, radical change, the kind of change which makes for an enlightened mind, that is, a mind which no longer only and merely functions partially, and this when it needs to, but which also is meditative, truly silent. Only such change as this can rightly be called profound transformation of the mind. So-called transformation of the mind like that spoken about here and, as we shall see later, is talked about by Tobin Hart is not real transformation but rather mere movement from one point on the level of a partially functioning mind to another. There needs to be revolution for deep transformation in education, but this is not the transformation which is talked about in this statement.

1.22
Parker: [In postmodern education,] education and teacher-education institutions [become] less like departments of science and more like departments of literature.
Commentator: This statement simply reflects preference on the part of the speaker or writer for right rather than left-brain partial mind functioning. Both science and literature are products of a merely partially functioning mind. Beyond both, and beyond the stance of the writer of this statement is the truly meditative mind. In education, if there is to be the fully educated person, a description of which will be attempted in the last chapter of this book, there must be concern for and a valuing of the truly meditative mind and of appropriate behaviour related to such concern and valuing.

1.23
Parker: The postmodern person is ... numerous selves in different contexts, the identity-switcher: unknowable and non-existent except within a relationship. At the same time she or he is committed to a framework of self-chosen, self-created values and realities.
Commentator: The self is not anything real, but it is knowable. It is the known in all its forms, the "selves," the various identities it takes on. As such it is never existing, that is, living. Its commitment to a framework is commitment to something merely fashioned on the level of thought, and any values it chooses or creates are not related to what *is*, the living, the eternal, the unknown, hence, so to speak, not to real "realities" at all. All of this means that the "postmodern person" or any other partially functioning mind fashioned person is not anything real. For teachers merely to lead students to the creation of any such so-called person is ever to engage in activity not at all related to the living, that with which a truly meditative mind communes.

1.24
Parker: Postmodern ... students and lecturers will come to see ... ways of life, styles of being human, as a matter of choice rather than discovery.
Commentator: One who advocates any such coming "to see" is clearly on the level of the merely partially functioning mind. If there is awareness of the importance of the truly meditative, silent mind, then one can understand that there is a way of living related not merely to the making

of choices by a merely partially functioning mind but also to discovery on the part of mind in a truly meditative state of the worth of living in direct relationship to what *is*, the living, the absolute, the unknown which is unknowable. Revolution in education relates to awareness that there can be, besides partial functioning of the mind, the totally silent, quiet, meditative mind, and it also relates to time and place being made for teachers and students to enter into learning related to such awareness and to living out of that awareness.

1.25
Parker: As for curriculum, get rid of it .... Postmodern teachers will construct pedagogy out of local interests and concerns where worth and value is set within a narrative in which its players have a stake and a voice.
Commentator: As far as the partially functioning mind is concerned, to advocate a getting rid of curriculum is to show preference for subjectivity over objectivity, for right rather than left-brain thinking, for so-called intuition divorced from strict rationality. The relativity and arbitrariness of proceeding in accord with such advocacy might well mean abandonment of necessary rigorous thinking as regards, for example, science and technology. If, however, curriculum and the structure and planning related to it are of worth or of value on the level of a partially functioning mind, and some would argue that they indeed are, and even if those who defend rigorous, objective thinking in education are right to do so, any curriculum in the ordinary sense and partially functioning mind activity related to its design and execution have no place when teacher and students are learning in relationship to the truly meditative mind. This point will be made clear in what follows later in chapter two.

1.26
Parker: Postmodern modes of learning will ... give postmodern ... students and teachers an opportunity of self-creation, the end point of which will ... be what we might prefer to call a cultivated, literate, and ironic human being; a citizen of postmodernity.
Commentator: The self created by so-called postmodern learning might make for "a cultivated, literate, and ironic" so-called "human being," just as some other form of so-called learning related to a different pattern or ideology might create a so-called human being differently described. Any one of these selves, however, will not at all be related to the totally understanding, meditative mind, a mind whose intelligence is loving and rightly seeing, whose intelligence goes to the depths of things, a mind that is uncontaminated, uninfluenced, and unconditioned, thus pristine, pure,

and in communion with what *is*, the living, the eternal, which is the unknown that can never be known.

1.27

Parker: There are no universal problems; just *ad hoc, ad hominem* rhetorical manoeuvres of persuasion; strategic interventions within the textual structure of actual, living conversations.

Commentator: There is what is universally real, what *is*, the living, the actual, but no subjectivity opposed to objectivity, like that implied here, will ever directly relate to it, just as objectivity, whether opposed to subjectivity or not, is likewise not so related. The living is the absolute, and living related to awareness of it has nothing at all to do with the relativity and arbitrariness reflected in this statement, nor with the merely abstract universalism fashioned by an objectively thinking, partially functioning mind. Rather than education merely related to subjectivity or objectivity, or some effort to synthesize the two, there can be education for meditative mind awareness as regards living or relating matters, and for proper objective functioning as regards the time-related concerns of a proper science and technology. A place can be given also to the arts, but a place not related to the making of extravagant claims which are there when it is suggested that right-brain, partial functioning of the mind, so-called intuition, can give people deep meaning and purpose in life, that what is partial and merely time-related can relate to the whole, the eternal, the absolute.

1.28

Parker: The process from destruction to creation is the education of postmodernity.

Commentator: What is of the merely partially functioning mind, namely, some process or activity involving destruction and so-called creation, or some other, is not really, truly creative. Only the truly meditative mind is really creative, in that it alone has to do with the really new, that is, the unknown, rather than with the dead and gone, the known, the experienced. Only it relates to the moment to moment and day to day dying and living that make possible deep meditative mind insight and understanding. Education limited only and always to the level of the merely partially functioning mind means limited education, education related only to the partial, the fragmentary, the limited, the ideated, the symbolized, to merely intellectual left-brain and so-called intuitive right-brain understanding.

1.29
Hart: Entering into depth is ... an ... awakening of ourselves that enables an expanded perception .... Education is no different; the choice to open more deeply ... is always present.
Commentator: Choice has to do with a merely partially functioning mind, and so, though there might be on the part of a choosing mind, either a lack of so-called depth or greater so-called depth, there cannot be a relationship to the real depths of what is living, the absolute, the mystery which is the living unknown. A self that is more open is still self, and, so long as self is there in any form, open or closed, there cannot be depth of perception, perception when there is no observer at all, or when the observer is the observed. Then, there cannot either be education related, not just to a partially functioning mind, but to one which is truly meditative.

1.30
Hart: Wisdom traditions and transpersonal theory ... help to describe what human consciousness is and how our education can encourage its unfolding.
Commentator: So-called wisdom traditions and the so-called transpersonal theories we read about in so-called humanistic psychology do indeed merely relate to consciousness and self-consciousness. All awareness, however, is not consciousness; there can be awareness without self there being aware. Only when there is this awareness and the insight and understanding related to it, only when there is the truly meditative mind, this is to say, is there communion with the living, the absolute, the eternal. Only such awareness and such a mind relate to real wisdom, and only education related to these and not just to mere partial functioning of the mind can be said to be education for fullness of living and a real relationship to what is the really and fully human.

1.31
Hart: Sages and mystics seek an education ... for "bringing forth" the inner person.
Commentator: There is no inner person, that is, some Self deeper than, other than, self, the ego. To seek to bring forth what is unreal is engagement in futile, illusion-related activity. Wisdom of the truly meditative mind is not there when so-called sages seek. What they seek is merely projection from out of their own limited, partially functioning minds which are futilely striving to attain to the unlimited. For educators to imitate so-called sages and mystics in classrooms, in halls of learning, is to attempt to condition the minds of students with the false or the

illusory while all the while they think that they are assisting them in discovery of deep meaning and purpose in life. All this is activity of the illusioned, the blind, seeking to transmit illusion to others.

1.32
Hart: Krishnamurti ... says that education is not just transmitting a subject but "bringing about a change in your mind" .... Training for intelligence involves cultivating thinking.
Commentator: The change in the mind about which Krishnamurti speaks is not what this author means by change, not mere superficial transformation of the mind, that is, movement from one form or level of a partially functioning mind to another, from one mode of consciousness to another. Rather, in the case of Krishnamurti, the concern is radical revolution in the mind which implies awareness of the possibility of mind being totally silent, lovingly meditative, and not merely right or left-brain thinking or functioning. Intelligence for Krishnamurti is profound and not merely that implied here and related to a merely partially functioning mind, to thinking on this level of the mind. No training and no cultivation in the ordinary sense can lead one to profound, loving intelligence. This is to say that, if training and cultivation imply separation of the teacher from the learners, that is, imply a supposedly knowing self, the teacher, so-called guiding selves who do not yet know but are engaged in a process leading to their coming to know, namely, students, then training and cultivation will never result in minds being profoundly, lovingly intelligent.

1.33
Hart: The development of heartfulness begins to take us beyond self-interest and self-separateness.
Commentator: Self is there when there is right or left-brain partial mind functioning. To suggest that there should be movement away from what is said to be too much left-brain functioning, too much of the mind, to more right-brain functioning, that is, to more "heartfulness," is to stay totally within the whole spectrum of consciousness and to think that as a result of such movement there will be the possibility of fathoming mystery, understanding living truth, capturing something of the eternal, the unknowable. At the end of this movement, or as a result of it, there is no awareness which is not consciousness, no real silence of the mind, mind in communion with what *is*, the eternal, the unknown. For a teacher, in a classroom, to operate always and only in relationship to consciousness and forms of thinking related to it is for her or him never to describe to

students what communion with the real, the living, the eternal, the unknown really is.

1.34
Hart: Wisdom ... involves the capacity to listen and to translate the power of the intellect and the openness of the heart into appropriate form (action, attitude, etc.).
Commentator: To say this is to say that wisdom is related to a partially functioning mind, to functioning in relationship to a synthesis of left-brain, intellectual functioning, and right brain, heart-related functioning, and that it is related to activity prompted by such functioning. Real wisdom, however, is not related to a merely partially functioning mind in any form, not to any activity or aspect of a merely partially functioning mind. Real wisdom is related to awareness which is not consciousness, that is, meditative mind awareness, to communion of a truly meditative mind with the eternal, the living, the absolute, the immeasurable, the unknown. For educators to present students with so-called wisdom related to a merely partially functioning mind as that which can give depth of intelligence, profound insight, true purpose and meaning in life is to engage and to attempt to have others, specifically students, engage in illusion-related activities.

1.35
Hart: Wisdom involves discovering the nature of the Self ... finding access to ... our wise Self.
Commentator: If there is not any such real Self, and indeed there is not, but merely one invented by thought, by a merely partially functioning mind, then there is nothing real to discover in this regard, and no point in referring to a merely thought-related mind as wise. For educators to so-called "educate" in relationship, not to what is real but rather to illusion, hence to what is false, is to condition minds more and more with what are illusory fashionings of an inappropriately partially functioning mind.

1.36
Hart: Transformation [relates to our] becoming more uniquely who we are, and [has to do with our attaining] unity and communion ....
We actualize our ever expanding potential by transcending current self-structure.
Commentator: Striving to become what is a mere projection of an inappropriately partially functioning mind, what one supposes one really is, militates against one really being in communion with what *is*, the living, the eternal. The unity which a supposedly real but merely mind-

made Self can come to is not anything real, not a direct and true relation to that whole which is the living, the unknown, the real mystery which is the eternal. Merely to go from one self-made structure, a currently fashionable one perhaps, to another structure similarly made but thought of as different is to stay within the confines of consciousness, never at all to be aware with an awareness which is not that of consciousness, not at all related to the meditative mind which has to do with this nonconscious awareness. What is called actualization here, that which is so often talked about today, in general, and in educational circles in particular, as much as the so-called potential which is said to be actualized, relates to mere activity of a partially functioning mind in relation to the unreal, the merely mind-invented, the merely imagined. The transcendence spoken about here is not real and radical for it involves mere movement from one point in the whole of consciousness to another. Not at all is it a going beyond conscious awareness to deep awareness which is not consciousness. Rather it is movement from one form of a partially functioning mind to another, not a going beyond all partial mind functioning such that there can be the total silence of the truly meditative mind. What is needed in education today, in addition to rigorous and proper partial functioning of the mind in relation to science, technology, and the practicalities of living in time, and in addition to learning in relation to the development of artistic skills and abilities, to the appreciation of the arts, is concern for real transcendence and for all that it makes possible.

1.37

Hart: Information can [be] the portal into deep learning.
Commentator: Information cannot be a gateway to deep learning for information relates necessarily to a superficially, partially functioning mind. Information and a partially functioning mind, whether left or right brain, or an amalgam of the two, must be ended or stopped before there can be what is deep, and learning in relation to it. To suggest anything contrary, as is done in this statement, is wrongly to confuse time and the eternal, and a partially functioning with a truly meditative mind. It is wrong to strive to use time and a partially functioning mind to capture something of the timeless and the truly meditative mind. To entertain a statement like this one in educational settings is to keep company with illusion, the false, and for teachers to use it as a guide as regards their classroom activities would be ignorance on their part, as well as an ignorant, in the sense of unwitting, attempt to condition the minds of students with the false, the illusory.

1.38

Hart: When awareness is turned inward, we find the world of subjective experience, consciousness, and meaning ... this inward path inquires into the depth of what makes us human.

Commentator: This awareness is awareness as consciousness, with self there. Inward or outward movement within the whole of consciousness is movement in relation to what is superficial. It is to make extravagant claims to suggest that any movement within consciousness, from left to right-brain partial functioning, or from right to left, from mind to so-called heart or vice versa, from reasoning to reflection or intuition or vice versa, is movement to what is deep. Only a truly meditative mind communes with what is deep, the living, and the deep which is the living is not anything fashioned by a partially functioning mind, mind which can and only does deal in fragments, in parts. It is only meditative mind awareness and the understanding associated with it which can really be said to relate to real transformation, to revolution in educational circles, in classrooms, in halls of learning.

1.39

Hart: As Krishnamurti ... says, "intelligence uses knowledge" ... and this involves the capacity to think clearly.

Commentator: What is of importance as regards this statement by Krishnamurti is to understand what he meant by intelligence. Speaking as he always did out of a meditative mind when the matter was living or relating, he meant by "intelligence," loving, and not rational intelligence, intelligence directly related to awareness and understanding on the level of the truly meditative mind. Thus, such intelligence does not at all involve the capacity to think clearly. Thinking is always, ordinarily speaking at least, on the level of a partially functioning mind. When there is mind in a meditative state, this statement by Krishnamurti rightly says, mind can function partially, as when, for example, it must use knowledge, where knowledge is necessary, of value. One must not, however, confuse loving intelligence, intelligence on the level of the meditative mind with the rational intelligence which relates to a partially functioning mind. It is important to see the difference between the two, just as it is important to see the difference between time and the timeless, and that between a partially functioning mind and a truly meditative one. In education there must be concern for clarity and rigor in relation to knowledge and for the conscious awareness and partially functioning mind to which it relates, but of great importance also, and hence what must also be of great concern to educators is loving intelligence, as well as the awareness without consciousness and the truly meditative mind to which such intelligence relates.

1.40
Hart: An education that fosters intelligence ... refines the mind through critical and creative thinking ... and the cultivation of imagination.
Commentator: Loving intelligence, which teachers and students can foster, one might say, is not at all related to the left-brain critical thinking which is of exclusive concern to some in education today, nor is it at all related to the right-brain so-called creative thinking which others in education, like Stuart Parker and Tobin Hart, prize and into which they think students should be initiated. For teachers to strive to cultivate students' imagination as regards living or relating matters is for them to focus on and deal with what is unreal, the false, the illusory, rather than for them to discover, together with students, the importance of one directly facing, with mind in a truly meditative state, what *is*, the real, the living, the eternal, the unknown.

1.41
Hart: Interaction of the intuitive and the analytic ... is basic to the renewal of education and the cultivation of intelligence.
Commentator: Any such attempted integration amounts merely to effort to amalgamate left and right-brain partial functioning of the mind. Any exclusive emphasis on left or right-brain functioning, or any attempt to amalgamate the two, as is suggested in this statement, relates not to the new, the eternal, the living, but only to what is old and dead, the merely ideated or merely imagined. Any so-called renewal of education, like that referred to here, relates only to movement on the level of the partially functioning mind, within the whole field of awareness which is consciousness. It has nothing at all to do with that real transformation or revolution in the mind which is there when mind stops all of its inappropriate partial functioning, and when there is then deep, real silence of the meditative mind. Merely to cultivate partial functioning mind intelligence, or something called such but really is not, will not and cannot make for that loving intelligence which is there when there is mind in a truly meditative state.

1.42
Hart: We bring intuition close through ... meditation ... dreams, imagination, stories.
Commentator: Though intuition or right-brain partial functioning of the mind is important as regards the development of left-brain thinking and its

related scientific theories and knowledge, and, though it is important in relationship to the arts, to artistic activities and endeavors, it has no place when the concern is living, relating. In these cases, meditation with a meditator, as much as dreams and stories, as well as imagination of what could, should, ought to, or might be, all of which are totally unrelated to what *is*, have no proper place at all. For teachers to engage students in activities and processes related to such is to do them a disservice, so to speak.

1.43
Hart: "Understanding" ... opens the door to a richer perception that transforms ... the self who is perceiving.
Commentator: One does well to see the proper place for intellectual understanding on the level of a partially functioning mind, and to see when what is appropriate is the integral, loving intelligence which is of a truly meditative mind. One also does well when one sees the difference between intellectual understanding and meditative mind intelligence. There is perception with perceiver there, and this is appropriate, even necessary, when the matter at hand properly relates to a partially functioning mind, but there is also perception without perceiver from out of a truly meditative mind. Any so-called transformation, however, which has to do with a mind-made merely perceiving self would not at all relate to profundity of understanding, to the richness which is the living, the absolute, the eternal, the real mystery which cannot be known. Any education which seeks merely to transform the self would be very limited, and, if the self is believed to be something actually or ultimately real, then there is that which is the false, the illusory.

1.44
Hart: Krishnamurti ... says .... "First of all you have to establish a relationship with the student ... first have affection."
Commentator: What one can ask here is what Krishnamurti's concern was when he talked about the establishment of such a relationship. He did not merely mean to suggest that it is important as regards proper partial functioning of the minds of students, but that it is very important or highly significant as regards a teacher's concern that students be meditatively aware, and as regards her or his expending energy so that theirs be loving intelligence and a direct relationship with what *is*, the living.

1.45
Hart: Education for character is ... about developing wholeness, a self undivided.

Commentator: It is a truly meditative mind which relates to actual, real wholeness, that is, the living, what *is*. When a partially functioning mind has a concern for wholeness, this wholeness is not the living but rather something merely abstract, that which is projected out of itself and called wholeness. A so-called undivided self is not fundamentally different from a divided self for both are not real but rather mere fashionings on the part of a partially functioning mind. If education for character is related to mere fashionings of a partially functioning mind, indeed related to what is unreal, even illusory, then of what worth is it? Rather than education for character there can be education for meditative mind awareness, awareness which involves a real relationship to the real, the living, the eternal, the new, the absolute, the immeasurable, and not merely to image, symbol, idea, and concept.

1.46

Hart: Education for wisdom and transformation is not about being taught but about waking up. Waking up requires ... capacities for taking the world into our consciousness.

Commentator: In this statement, "taught" likely refers to left-brain partial mind functioning and "waking up" to right-brain partial mind functioning. "Transformation" could be said to mean movement from left-brain to right-brain mind functioning, and what is there at the end and as a result of this movement is supposedly wisdom, a state of awakened consciousness. Real wisdom or real awakening are there, however, not when there is merely movement of some kind within the whole of consciousness, movement from one form of a partially functioning mind to another, but rather when, neither in opposition to proper rational nor to any improper irrational partial functioning of the mind, there is awareness which is not consciousness, which is other than consciousness, when there is, this is to say, a truly meditative state of mind. Education related to concern for real wisdom, for truly significant transformation of the mind, therefore, is quite different from what is being suggested in this statement.

1.47

Hart: As we tap into the realms of Self, we may gain access to a wide range of sources of information and guidance.

Commentator: Any so-called information and guidance resulting from a tapping into realms of the Self, that is, a supposed real self, would be false information, neither knowledge nor meditative mind wisdom for the Self is not anything real but rather only a projection from out of thought, out of an inappropriately partially functioning mind. For the mind of a student to be unduly conditioned by a teacher along the lines of what is suggested in this statement is for her or him to follow what is false, for him or her not to have been rightly guided but rather misguided. If and when teachers present false information, that is, what is neither knowledge nor sound, reasoned opinion to students, or when they attempt to lead or guide them along paths leading to illusion, surely it can be said that they, even if unwittingly, are acting out of ignorance, and what they are doing cannot be condoned, cannot have any real worth or value.

1.48
Hart:　　　　　　I have found it powerful ... to invite students on a search for their wise Self through the gateway of the imagination. All kinds of activities help, from journal writing to creating stories, to meditation.
Commentator:　　To encourage students to engage themselves in any search for Self, so-called wise or not, is to encourage them to engage in futile activity. Any such search has to do with looking for what is unreal, what is something merely projected out of someone's imaginative, perhaps speculating but nevertheless partially functioning mind. As regards living or relating, imagination can only be a pathway to falsehood, to illusion. For teachers to condition the minds of students so that they engage themselves in the kinds of activities mentioned here can only be said to be wrong and ill-advised.

1.49
Hart:　　　　　　Concepts of inner wisdom and the wise Self are found throughout ... wisdom traditions and in ... personal experience, but they are not entertained in mainstream education largely because of the underestimation of the Self.
Commentator:　　What is lacking in mainstream education is not what is said here to be of value, that is, a proper estimation of the Self for the Self is not anything real. What is lacking in mainstream, but also in fringe education, is awareness of the importance of understanding on the level of the truly meditative mind. All is partially functioning mind related only, either left or right-brain related, or related to some attempted synthesis of the two.

1.50
Hart:　　　　　　Meditation has proven to be extremely enduring and helpful because it provides a structured practice through which to develop and refine awareness.
Commentator:　　There is ignorance, illusion-related practice when teachers "teach" meditation, when they strive to initiate students into their own or someone else's, perhaps some so-called spiritual authority's, some

mystic's partially functioning mind fashioned "structured" practices. Such striving is merely the attempt unduly to condition minds. The result of such striving might be a so-called intensification of consciousness but not at all anything related to transformation of the mind such that there is awareness which is not consciousness and that to which such awareness relates, the real, the living.

1.51
Hart: One [can come to recognize] the "I" .... as distinct from the contents of consciousness .... As we center ourselves in the "I," we gain the ability to see more clearly .... Thoughts, feelings ... can then be claimed as ours, but they are not us.
Commentator: There is no "I" distinct from the contents of consciousness. These contents are the "I," and this whether the "I" is merely self or ego, or a so-called higher Self. There is no clarity of mind when one centers the mind on something unreal, thinking as one does so that one is in relationship with something real, something living. It is only when one is aware that thoughts and feeling are what we are, that is, what our partially functioning minds are, that there is that depth of awareness and understanding which are not there in education as we generally see it today.

1.52
Hart: The ... function of education [is] cultivating the whole being, the totality of mind.
Commentator: Left and right-brain partial functioning of the mind do not together make for the whole human being, the totality of mind. While it would be wrong for teachers to seek to engage students in improper partial mind functioning, it is a too limited education which merely seeks to cultivate proper left and right-brain partial mind functioning . It is only when there is concern that theirs be meditative mind awareness and meditative mind insight and understanding, that theirs be wisdom on the level of a truly meditative mind, as well as properly developed partially functioning minds that there is education for the whole human being, for the totality of mind. Even when there is concern for what is said to be deep feeling of the soul as talked about by poets and mystics, what is talked about relates merely to a right-brain partially functioning mind and not at all to the totality of mind. Such talk does not relate to a mind which properly functions partially when this is necessary but otherwise is totally silent, truly meditative. Rather it relates to illusion, to the false belief that what is called the soul is something real.

1.53

Hart: [When] education is ... an opportunity to ... deepen consciousness, [its] aims ... reach beyond information exchange to transformation.

Commentator: Any deepening of consciousness is not profound transformation of the mind. Such transformation is not any movement from one point or aspect of a merely partially functioning mind to another, perhaps from left to right-brain functioning, that is, what is implied here to be proper or desirable. Beyond information exchange, that is, left-brain partial functioning of the mind, but also beyond the right-brain functioning being suggested here as transformation of the mind is meditative mind awareness. Only when there is education for such awareness and not just for partially functioning mind intelligence and understanding is there education related to real transformation rather than for mere movement from one point within the whole of consciousness to another.

Such, then, are examples of the limitations, indeed the falseness of much that one reads in educational books and journals. In the next chapter we turn to what could be said to be a negation of these limitations and falsehoods such that relative to education there then comes an understanding of and insight into what could be said to be real revolution in education.

Chapter Two

Teaching, Learning, and the Fully Functioning Meditative Mind

> There is no path to wisdom. If there is a path, then wisdom is the formulated; it is already imagined, known ... wisdom [cannot] be known or cultivated.
>
> One can live very happily when no importance is given to the self; and this also is part of right education.
>
> J. Krishnamurti

It can be said that in what is quoted in this chapter from Krishnamurti's, *A Flame of Learning*,[1] and in the accompanying commentary, there is a call for radical revolution in education. It would be wrong, however, to portray such a call as a suggested alternative to proper and appropriate partial functioning of the mind. The call is to go deep, to the level of the truly meditative mind, that level of mind where there are no opposites, no alternatives.

If there is realization of the value of and need for meditative mind awareness, then, quite naturally, as regards education, the "how" question arises. How can a teacher in a classroom proceed so that there might be awakening of the deeper level of the minds of students, the awakening of that level of the mind which is other than merely partially functioning, awakening of the level of the truly silent, really quiet, meditative mind? In this chapter we first of all read Krishnamurti's posing of the "how" question and commentary on what he says, and then in the latter part of the chapter we read some of what Krishnamurti says relative to providing an adequate answer to this question. Again, there is accompanying commentary. First, then, we turn to the question.

The "How" Question

2.0
Krishnamurti: As educators ... are we not trying ... to awaken ... intelligence? [As educators,] how [can we] create that intelligence [which enables one] to deal with life, [which makes for learners who are] intelligent, in the classroom and outside the classroom?
Commentator: What one must understand when this statement is read is what Krishnamurti means by awakening, by intelligence, and by learning. Awakening relates to meditative mind awareness and not just awareness which is consciousness on the level of a merely partially functioning mind. It relates to intelligence which is loving and not merely rational, to awareness which is not consciousness, and to a mind which is really silent, not merely to conscious awareness and to a left or a right-brain partially functioning mind. It is loving intelligence which is appropriate as regards living or relating, communion with the living, the eternal, the unknown, and a merely partially functioning mind intelligence which correctly relates, as in the case of science, for example, to time, the known, the experienced, the recognized. Krishnamurti's is a call for educators to do more than they now generally do, namely, to have a concern and a love for not only a properly but partially functioning mind but also for a truly meditative one, and for them to expend energy in communicating this concern and love to students.

2.1
Krishnamurti: When I say 'how,' I do not mean a method, a system, or a structure ... not a way [but rather] how to proceed.
Commentator: This statement reflects a clear and correct understanding of the difference between conscious awareness and awareness which is other than conscious awareness and of the difference between a partially functioning and a fully functioning, truly meditative mind. Methods, systems, and structures properly relate to a partially functioning mind but not to a meditative one. Part of what educators could rightly do is communicate these differences to students as well as the implications for living related to an understanding of them. Some suggestions as to how a teacher can proceed to do this are presented later in the second half of this chapter.

2.2

Krishnamurti: These two working together, awakening of intelligence and order, at the same time, so that there is no disorder [is important]. How shall we work together, teach each other and the student, to bring this about?

Commentator: Krishnamurti here is asking the question of the proper procedure for the awakening of loving intelligence and the order in living or in relating which is there when there is truly the state of the meditatorless meditative mind. He is not, as was said earlier, asking for partially functioning mind related methods to effect such awakening. He is here talking to teachers and asks them how they can assist each other as well as those they teach to have minds which commune with the real, the living, the eternal. A truly meditative mind is never confused, hence is never disordered. A disordered partially functioning mind is possible when, rather than its partial functioning being rational, it is irrational, when there is movement away from rational functioning of the mind into the illusion or the falseness which a so-called intuitive or mystical, merely imaginative or speculating mind can and so often does create.

2.3

Krishnamurti: Before [students] plunge into subjects, [the teacher can talk] to them about ... awakening of intelligence and order.

Commentator: Here, Krishnamurti's use of the word "before" indicates that, though in a classroom in which by intent there is a focus on some particular subject matter, like mathematics or science, there can be talking about the importance or the significance of a truly meditative mind, and of things properly related to it, there will not be any attempt to confuse, for example, the level of the mind which properly relates to mathematics or to science with the level of the meditative mind, that level of the mind which has to do with loving intelligence and the total mind order which is possible when there is this intelligence. The teacher will be clear about the difference between time and the timeless. She or he will understand that the first cannot lead to the second, and that it is not any engagement in activities properly related to the actual learning of particular subject matter, nor in any other activity related to partial mind functioning, which will lead to awakening of the truly meditative mind.

2.4

Krishnamurti: The intention of [Krishnamurti] schools is to impart ... Krishnamurti's teachings ... to the students through their [academic] subjects .... To teach the ordinary subjects is essential for various reasons

... but can we, through the subjects which every student has to go through, convey these teachings to them?

Commentator: Because of the dualism of time and the timeless, the necessity of time ceasing before the timeless can be, and because this was something which Krishnamurti clearly understood, the last part of this statement cannot mean that teachers should attempt to use an academic subject as a vehicle to acquire the level of the mind to which Krishnamurti's writings relate, namely, the truly meditative one. If teachers were to attempt so to use any academic subject, this would be a turning of the subject into something which it is not, and it would be doing something like trying, futilely, to use the known to reach the unknowable. What these words could mean is that in a classroom in which a particular subject is being taught there are times when the teacher will say, for example, and speaking figuratively, "Let us now climb the ladder," or "Let us dive down into the deep," meaning, let us stop the partially functioning mind activity in which we have been engaged, for example, examining, thinking about, and discussing what thinkers and writers have said about what freedom is, or the concept or notion of freedom talked about in some particular book. "Let's look now at some of the things Krishnamurti says about freedom. What is the difference between what he says about freedom and the notion of freedom in the book we have been studying? What about your life? Is it free in Krishnamurti's sense of freedom?" And so, as Krishnamurti himself puts it, teacher and students together "go into" things along the lines being suggested here. To emphasize, what has just been presented here is merely one example of how a teacher with a concern and a love for the truly meditative mind might proceed in a classroom.

2.5

Krishnamurti: [An academic subject] is a medium.

Commentator: Again, one must not take this as suggesting a mixing up of an academic subject and all of the things related to the teaching and learning of such with description of and talk about, in a classroom, meditative mind awareness and all of its implications. To do so would be to confuse the timeless with what can properly be related to time, to confuse nonconscious awareness with conscious awareness, and to confuse a totally functioning with a partially functioning mind. Since, however, the partially functioning mind and one which is truly silent are not opposite one to the other, and, since the former is the part and the latter the whole, and there need be no opposition between the part and the whole, there can be harmony in relation to the part or parts, and in relation to the whole, in relation to the partially functioning and to the fully functioning mind. Harmony is there when totality of the mind is there, with partial mind functioning whenever this is necessary or appropriate but not when such functioning can create confusion and conflict.

As Krishnamurti says, it is important that there be "harmony" in relation to "the known and the unknown,"[2] that is, not a partially functioning mind effected harmony of parts, or fragments, be they left or right-brain related, but harmony in living such that there is ever-present meditative mind awareness and partial functioning of the mind when, but only when, necessary. There must not be, this is to say, undue mixing up of what properly relates to the limited with the unlimited, must not be confusion of the measurable with the immeasurable, of the known with the unknown, an attempt to blend, synthesize, or amalgamate the partial and the whole, the known and the unknown, an effort to effect a merely mind-fashioned integration or harmony.

When there is no conflict at all, when there is the total functioning of the truly meditative mind, there is harmony in living and no conflict fashioned by some fragment of the mind opposing some other fragment or causing conflict as it attempts to become the whole. Real wholeness relates only to the unknown, the real, the living, the eternal and not at all to the known, the ideal, the merely temporal, in relation to which there can be partial mind related activity but not the action of love which alone can be communion with the living, the real, the eternal.

Harmony in relation to the known and the unknown is something which teachers and students can learn about in a classroom. In mathematics, for example, there can be discovery that just as there is great order in mathematics so there is great order in the universe and in a mind which is truly meditative. In history, there can be the discovery, for example, of the disharmony and conflict created by minds which were always and only partially functioning, often irrationally so, discovery that the same disharmony that can be seen in history is there in the lives of people today, that, whenever there is conflict in the mind, then one's mind is the same as that of someone read about in history books.

To consider, at appropriate times, in a classroom, the limits of a particular science being studied so as correctly to see what science can and cannot do, to see that science is not related to the absolute but rather is a time-related pursuit, that it can only relate to the known and the knowable unknown, but not ever to the mystery which is the unknowable unknown is for minds, those of the teacher and the students, to explore and discover what is the whole and what is merely a part, and the proper relation of mind to both the whole and the part or parts. A similar thing could be done when literature is taught and learned in a classroom. When, for example, there is study of a piece of poetry, the teacher can point out that the poem is a creation of a partially functioning mind, is the expression of an experience reflected upon and cast into poetic form. In addition to the partially functioning mind understanding which results from a study of the imagery used to express the experience, there could be a teacher's description of and discovery by students of the limits of all expression, a making clear that any description of an experience, like the experience itself, is related to the past and not to actual experiencing of the living, the eternal, the new and alive, mystery which is unknowable.

To reiterate, in a classroom set up for partial functioning mind teaching and learning of an academic subject, there can be times when there is not, to speak figuratively, merely a shifting of gears but rather a stopping of the engine and a stepping out of the car so as quietly to look at the beautiful flowers and trees along the roadside. Only when there is a complete cessation of movement or of activity on the part of a partially functioning mind can there be awareness of and communion with what *is*, that is, the living, rather than the merely abstract images and symbols, ideas and concepts fashioned by such mind functioning.

2.6

Krishnamurti: I would not talk about [Krishnamurti's] teachings. I am concerned ... about the transformation of a human mind, human being, which is absolutely necessary in this culture, or in these times. That is all we are concerned about, not about Krishnamurti's teachings. To blazes with all that .... I would not enter into that at all. I say: are we concerned about this, are we passionate about this. It has nothing to do with somebody's teaching.

Commentator: If teachers and students in a classroom read and "go into" some of the writings of Krishnamurti, these must not be used as authoritative words, as the words of the Bible or of a so-called master of the spiritual life are often used. Any description is never the described. Limitation of words in relation to both levels of the mind, partially and fully functioning, can be "gone into" in a classroom. It is this kind of consideration, perhaps, that Krishnamurti was concerned about when he made the statement here quoted. Krishnamurti's or someone else's talk to communicate something relative to words spoken and written in an effort to describe meditative mind awareness, total freedom, and selfless love are not at all the same as a mind which is truly meditative, totally free, and selflessly loving. This is an important understanding for teachers and learners learning what is right living, right relating.

2.7
Krishnamurti: If we ... think [Krishnamurti's] teachings are important, how shall we transmit them to the student so that we have a different kind of human being leaving these schools who is not just like everybody else?
Commentator: What is clear, given the real dualism of time and the timeless, and the real difference between them, as well as the consequent difference between the superficial mind's state of awareness and that of the deep, meditative mind, is not only that the latter awareness relates to fullness of humanity while the former merely to what "everybody's" humanity is ordinarily or usually thought to be, but also that teaching and learning in relation to these two different states of the mind are different. A teacher's way of proceeding is different, as will be suggested later in this chapter, depending on which level of mind is the concern of the teacher and the students. These important differences are not seen by people like, for example, Stuart Parker and Tobin Hart, who, as we have seen, wrongly think that a partially functioning mind can develop into a truly meditative one, that there can be continuity as regards movement from partial to total functioning of the mind rather than a stopping of all movement on the part of a partially functioning mind in order that the mind be truly meditative. Though there can be no such continuity, this does not mean there must be disharmony as regards the two levels. There will be no disharmony if there is clarity of understanding of the nature but also of the difference between a partially functioning and a fully functioning, truly meditative mind.

2.8
Krishnamurti: I feel very strongly that [students] should radically change psychologically. That is my chief concern, nothing else, except they have to study, and all that. But my chief concern, my commitment, my passion, is that when they leave here they should be totally different human beings. That is my chief concern.
Commentator: This statement of Krishnamurti clearly states that full and proper education must relate both to partially functioning mind awareness and thinking as well as to meditative mind awareness and living. Radical psychological change is possible only when there is not only a properly and appropriately partially functioning mind but also one that is meditative. For students to have fully developed, highly rational and appropriately intuitive minds they "have to study, and all that." But for students to be "totally different human beings," ones whose intelligence is not only rational, but loving, ones whose minds are totally unconditioned, psychologically speaking, hence really free, their minds must be truly meditative. Only an education which goes beyond aims

related to proper development of partially functioning minds, a going beyond related to discovery of the truly meditative state of mind, is education related to human beings who are totally different from what they usually or ordinarily are.

2.9

Krishnamurti: I would like to teach the student [something] I am very interested in, [which is] something that to me is of the greatest importance, [for example, unconditioning of the mind, real freedom of the mind], with all the implications of behaviour, responsibility, relationship, all that is involved in it. I would like to convey this to the student and I want him to live it as I am trying to live it, so that we both are on the same level in discussing with each other, so we understand each other.

Commentator: This statement clearly relates to concern for truly meditative mind awareness and the significant understanding and insight which are possible when there is such awareness. Here, "teaching" and "conveying" must be understood in relationship to such awareness and not to the conscious awareness implied when there is the merely partially functioning mind and any either right or left-brain related academic subject or discipline, any one of the arts or the sciences. Conscious awareness in relationship to partially functioning mind teaching and learning gives rise to methods, strategies, structures, teachers separate from learners and vice versa, and so on, but all these would militate against what is appropriate and proper when there is teaching and learning in relationship to meditative mind awareness. More about this will be said in the last part of this chapter.

2.10

Krishnamurti: How am I, if I am a teacher ... to convey to the student what behaviour is, through my subject throughout the day?

Commentator: When there is concern for behaviour, the concern is proper if related to right living, right relating, that is, holism in living rather than fragmentation of living, having to do with what is real, the living, rather than with images and concepts, hence unreal fashionings by a partially functioning mind. Putting this matter in different words, one can say that right concern for behaviour relates to the truly meditative mind rather than the partial mind functioning which is proper when it has to do with science, technology, the practicalities of living, works of art, and so on. Teachers and students, in a classroom in which a particular academic subject is taught, can "go into" what right behaviour is, but there must not be, as has already been suggested, undue or unwarranted confusion of the timeless with what is merely time-related, of awareness which is not consciousness with conscious awareness, of a partially functioning with a fully functioning mind.

2.11

Krishnamurti: [There can be] learning about relationship, learning about fear, about the many psychological factors, and also about all the various human endeavours in different fields, [learning] about as many things as [one] can.

Commentator: This statement could be said to be a call by Krishnamurti for total functioning of the mind, for learning on the level of a partially functioning mind and for learning as related to a meditative mind. The former kind of learning relates to "endeavours in different fields" and is necessary for ordered living in relation to time. Learning in relationship to psychological matters, to right living, right relating, however, is learning in relationship to a truly silent, meditative mind. Concern for revolution in the mind is there in education when there is concern, on the part of the teacher and the students, not only for full development of the rational and intuitive aspects of a partially functioning mind but also concern for the deeper mind, so to speak, the mind which is able not only to function partially when this is necessary but to function totally and make for holistic rather than fragmentary living.

2.12

Krishnamurti: [It is important for students] to be academically trained ... but let us give much more emphasis to [psychological matters, to relationships].

Commentator: Again, here, there is expression of the value of and the need for education related to teachers and students being concerned about and working together for total functioning of the mind, for engagement not only in necessary or appropriate partial right and left-brain functioning of the mind but also for deep meditative mind awareness. It should be obvious that the necessity and value of the advancement of science demands right-brain intuition, what Einstein referred to as imagination, to guide and advance the progress of scientific knowledge. This necessity and this value, however, should not lead one to deny or ignore the value of the truly meditative mind for only such a mind relates to discovery of meaning in living. Such discovery is impossible if one follows those who resort to greater emphasis on right-brain rather than left-brain partial mind functioning because they think this is the appropriate way of approaching and dealing with living, that is, relating, matters. What they actually so often do is make exaggerated, indeed false claims relative to the discovery of that meaning in living which is there when mind is in a truly meditative state.

2.13

Krishnamurti: [It is important] to come off the superficial level.

Commentator: In educational settings, it is important for teachers and students to operate on the superficial level of the mind, in relation to the pursuit of knowledge in the sciences and the development of skill and ability in the arts, for the highest possible development of appropriate left and right-brain partial mind functioning. For teachers and students to stay only and always on this level of the mind, however, is for them ever to face the merely limited – the known, the experienced, the abstract, time and things which are related to time – and never to move beyond this level to that of the truly meditative mind, where there can be direct communion with the real, the new, the living, the eternal, the mystery which is the unknown, so that there can be that harmony in living which is possible when there is full functioning of the mind, that is, mind functioning partially when such functioning is appropriate but otherwise being silent, truly meditative. If there were to be real revolution in education and truly significant transformation in the lives of teachers and students, there would not just be concern for and thinking related to a partially functioning mind but also concern for and experiencing of the state of the truly meditative mind and of all that is possible once there is this state of mind. This would include the living of a deeply meaningful life, with real joy, profound peace, immeasurable order, and real harmony as regards time and as regards the timeless, the known and the unknown, of a mind which functions partially when it needs to but which otherwise is always and profoundly silent.

2.14

Krishnamurti: Being a teacher ... how would I transform ... children and myself, basically? That would be my chief interest. And I would also like them to have first class intellects and fully developed minds, the whole totality of entity. In what way am I to proceed in doing that? How shall I, as a teacher, set about transformation of students psychologically and also have them be academically capable, efficient? ... How do I approach this whole problem with the student, knowing that the student is very conditioned, resisting? ... I am really, deeply, passionately interested in this. [There must be] no motive ... only then [can we] cooperate ... I have to learn ... with the students' [and other teachers' help], to lose my self-interest, the desire to dominate and all that, which are forms of self-interest.

Commentator: This statement points to Krishnamurti's profound understanding of the nature of the human mind, relates to his awareness that besides functioning partially the mind can be absolutely, totally quiet, silent, and in its silence in communion with what *is*, the eternally living. He does not at all suggest that there should be less rational and more intuitive mind functioning as is suggested, for example, by Stuart Parker and Tobin Hart. There should be, rather, rigorously and critically thinking minds in relation to science and technology, for example, and appropriate right-brain functioning, as for example, in relation to literature and the fine arts. Krishnamurti does not at all make the extravagant, indeed false claims made by those who suggest that more right and less left-brain partial functioning of the mind or some kind of synthesis of right and left-brain functioning can give deep meaning and purpose in living, can make for right living, right relating. Krishnamurti is well aware that it is only meditative mind awareness which relates to right living, right relating, and that only when there is such awareness is there real psychological transformation in the human mind.

Krishnamurti's talk about transformation of teachers and students shows that the usual, partially functioning mind separation of teacher from learners is appropriate when there is concern for the development of "first class intellects," but not when the concern or matter is the meditative mind. Emphasis in this regard is given by Krishnamurti when he says that the teacher has "to learn ... with the students ... to lose ... all ... forms of self-interest." In what follows now, more is said about the difference between teaching and learning in relationship to a partially functioning mind and teaching and learning in relationship to the truly meditative mind.

Answers to the "How" Question

2.15
Krishnamurti: [As a teacher] I do not want to influence; that to me is a drug. It is for [each one of us, including each student] to see [the matter] for [oneself], and therefore it is finished, I do not have to tell you [or him or her]. Can we, [that is, we teachers and students] together see this? *Together*, not I see it and you do not see it, and therefore when you see it, you influence me, and you tell me what to do. To see this together. If we see it, or when we see it, or are learning to see it – that is better, learning to see it – in the very act of learning to see it, how do we convey this to the student? I think we convey it when we are passionate about something.

Commentator: If influence means undue conditioning of the mind, then it can be said that any such influence is antithetical not only as regards proper development of a partially functioning mind, but that it also is antithetical, so to speak, to a mind in a truly meditative state. Undue conditioning of the mind is inappropriate not only as regards meditative mind teaching and learning but also as regards proper partially functioning mind teaching and learning. When the matter is properly either left or right-brain partially functioning mind related, then the teacher, as the one who already knows a particular subject matter, can, by appropriate methods and procedures, and with justification, seek to initiate students into a right understanding of such subject matter, some aspect of an academic discipline. When, however, the matter is living related, then as Krishnamurti says here, the student must see for himself or herself just as the teacher must do so. It could be said that in this case each one, whether the teacher of some subject matter or a student learning this subject matter, is both the teacher and the learner. When, together, they are exploring and discovering something about right living, there is the possibility of each one totally understanding this something in relationship to that supreme intelligence, insight, and wisdom which come only to a truly meditative mind.

2.16

Krishnamurti: [When,] in talking about [living or relating] to the student, [about] what it means in [his or her, that is, in the teacher's own] life, [the teacher is] learning about it; therefore it is affecting [this teacher's] life.

Commentator: The learning talked about here is on the level of the truly meditative mind. It has nothing at all to do with a partially functioning mind coming to an understanding of accumulations and gatherings in either a left or a right-brain partially functioning mind, has nothing to do with theories, ideas, and concepts of a mathematical or scientific kind, for example, nor with the theme and plot development of a piece of literature, or the images and symbols in a poem. Neither has it to do with teacher and students merely expressing and so-called sharing their so-called personal opinions, reasoned or not, in the way which is done in many classrooms which are not those in which the so-called hard sciences are taught. It rather is learning related to understanding now of the now, the living, the eternal, the unknown, the ever new and never continuous. The learning, in this case, is therefore learning as one is living rather than merely thinking, is learning related to meditative mind awareness, that is, learning not in relation to contents of the conscious mind fashioned by either left or right-brain partial mind functioning but rather learning from everything as one goes along in life, moment to moment, day to day.

2.17

Krishnamurti: [As a teacher,] the first thing I want [students] to understand [is the importance of listening] to what I am saying .... As this is my chief concern, I would meet them every day about that. I would set apart ten minutes, or a quarter of an hour every day and say, 'Listen now, we must find out together how to change ourselves, radically.' I would say, 'Are you interested in this? Do you want this to happen?' Then they would ask me, 'What do you mean by change?' Then I would have a dialogue with them. Then, in that dialogue we [would] show each other how we are conditioned, how we accept things, and so on, and so on. I would devote my energies to this quarter of an hour completely to make them understand it .... Because I feel passionately, I would convey my passion to them.

Commentator: This passage points to a number of important understandings related to learning on the level of the truly meditative mind. Deep listening is listenerless, and what this means and the significance of it are two things which the teacher can and would "go into" in the ten minutes or quarter of an hour mentioned in this quoted passage. This ten or fifteen minutes would relate to teacher and students being on the deep level of the mind where, strictly speaking, there is no difference between teacher and students but rather the teacher and the students are together examining, learning about living or right relating rather than in relationship to some particular subject matter or academic discipline. The other minutes in the period devoted to study of subject matter would relate to the superficial level of the mind, either left or right-brain, depending on the kind of subject matter being taught by the teacher and learned by the students.

Strictly speaking, dialogue implies people holding to their own or a group's specific, partially functioning mind derived conclusions even as they strive to understand and to a measured degree cooperate with others to establish some level of toleration for beliefs and values different from their own. It is not dialogue in this sense of covering over of differences in thinking and in living with a blanket of toleration about which Krishnamurti is speaking when here he talks about dialoguing for his concern is meditative mind awareness and not the merely conscious awareness which is at play on the part of parties to a dialogue of the usual or ordinary kind.

2.18

Krishnamurti: I may convey [love] to you if you are very quiet. Instead of all these arguments, back and forth, perhaps if you are very quiet, you may know of it, I may convey it to you, or ... there might be non-verbal communication .... I want that for ... students .... My concern is that, nothing else.

Commentator: This is clearly a statement made from out of a truly meditative mind, and the concern is for the silence related to such a mind rather that the talk, perhaps the argumentation, which is at times appropriate in a classroom when there is partial functioning of the mind related to the pursuit of some academic discipline. Communication on the level of a partially functioning mind, and related, in an educational setting, to talk, discussion, and transmission of ideas and concepts or to an understanding of images and symbols which are there in works of art, related respectively to the sciences or the arts, this is to say, implies separation between the one who communicates subject matter and those who receive the communication, that is, the teacher and the students respectively. When the teacher and the students in a classroom have transcended the level of the partially functioning mind to which such communication relates, they are then on the level of communion. Communication, then, can be out of love rather than out of thought, out of the silence which is there when there is the loving intelligence of mind in a truly meditative state.

2.19

Krishnamurti: [As it is now, young people] go to all the various schools and colleges to be conditioned, more and more. If they can condition them, I do not see why you cannot uncondition them.

Commentator: Some conditioning of the partially functioning mind is necessary and of value, and this when, for example, there must be learning of research methods, proper procedures, and efficiency regarding some partially functioning mind related mechanical operation. Other conditioning, for example, related to matters psychological, that is to living-related matters, is not only unnecessary but detrimental or harmful as regards ordered living. Here Krishnamurti is talking to teachers. His call is for a concern on their part for meditative mind awareness in students for it is only such which can make for a mind which is utterly, totally unconditioned, psychologically speaking. He is urging these teachers to consider the importance of their cultivating minds which, in relationship to living, are totally unconditioned and how they might go about making such awareness not only their own but that of students.

2.20
Krishnamurti: Go into the problem of ... blocks. Help [students] to get rid of those ... blocks and let the river flow to carry everything away.

Commentator: Unconditioning of the mind, freeing it, psychologically speaking, from the past, from unnecessary and harmful so-called authoritative influences of every kind, be they psychological or so-called spiritual, from experiences of a psychological and so-called spiritual kind, from the known, psychologically speaking, is what Krishnamurti is talking about here. When, in a classroom, the concern and the talk is on the level of the truly meditative mind, the teacher and the students together can discover, can choicelessly and observerlessly see and so understand, have insight into the conditionings of their own minds for what they are and be free of them. Theirs can be the wisdom which is there when there is communion with what actually, really *is*, the eternally living. When there is this communion rather than living in relationship to the ideal, the unreal, the wished for, the merely imagined and speculated upon, then, psychologically speaking, the river flows, so to speak. It is ever washing away the dead and gone, psychological memories, and then the new, the unknown, the fresh, the pure and innocent, all that is not touched and contaminated by wrongly partially functioning minds stands out in all its resplendency, there to be communed with in the state of the fully functioning, truly meditative mind.

2.21
Krishnamurti: [As a teacher, I say to students,] let us work this out in life .... They get hurt, they feel uncomfortable, they are frightened. So you have to go into it, point it all out. You are making them uncomfortable, so is life making them uncomfortable.

Commentator: Really to work things out in life is observerlessly to see, to observe from out of a really quiet, silent mind. When there is such seeing, there is deep understanding, hence a "solving" of any problem of living which is there because of wrong partial mind functioning. Partial functioning of the mind is of value when the concern, for example, is mathematics or science but not when it causes psychological chaos and disorder in the lives of people. Though unconditioning of the mind, of great concern to teachers and students when they are on the deep rather than the superficial level of the mind, may cause initial discomfort and even fright, the total understanding which comes from a going into all of the implications of undue mind conditioning means there will be dissipation of such discomfort or fright. The seriousness that must be there in any such "going into" is indicated in what Krishnamurti says in this statement of his.

2.22
Krishnamurti: I would approach [the matter of unconditioning the minds of students causing them to be hurt] in ten different ways. I would talk to them about meditation.
Commentator: This statement, it might be said, relates to what might be called the art of teaching and learning on the level of the meditative mind. Strictly speaking, of course, art and artistic endeavours, at least ordinarily or usually, are partially functioning mind related, hence imply self as artist and selves to appreciate and critique the products which result from these endeavours. Though the talk of a teacher who is concerned about the deep mind might be said to be on the level of the partially functioning mind, ultimately it comes from out of a truly silent one. The truly silent mind is utterly, totally unconditioned, speaking psychologically. It is the deep mind, and education which relates to the deep and not merely to the superficial is education related to real, revolutionary mind transformation.

2.23
Krishnamurti: They are children, they are young, they are sensitive; they are also conditioned, they are also hard, they have settled in a groove. [As a teacher] you have to pull them out of it. That might hurt, it all depends [on] how you deal with it.
Commentator: This clearly indicates that education related to the awakening of supreme intelligence, to full understanding of matters related to living has to do with deep, radical, complete unconditioning of the mind. Selfless "artistry," so to speak, is called for when teachers and students communicate with one another about conditioning and unconditioning of the mind. If there is merely "artistry" with self there rather than selfless "artistry," there will be motives and self-interests which militate against total, full unconditioning of the mind.

2.24
Krishnamurti: I would convey [the need for transformation,] but whether [the students] do something about it is a different matter. They [at least would] know what I am talking about.
Commentator: This statement makes clear that, as regards education for awakening of the truly meditative mind and for the communion with the living to which such a state of mind relates, everyone in a classroom, that is, the teacher and each student, is ultimately her or his own teacher and learner. There are no theories, ideas, or concepts, no images or symbols, no subject matter, this is to say, to be transmitted from the one who knows or supposedly knows, that is, the teacher, to the learners of the content, the

students. In any given classroom, it is possible that all minds, those of teacher and students, are on a truly meditative mind level, totally understanding matter related to living or relating, hence in communion with what *is*, the living. It is possible, too, however, that not all of the minds of students are on this level, or even that none of them are. Perhaps they may never be. It is these latter possibilities to which Krishnamurti is referring in this statement.

2.25

Krishnamurti: [As a teacher, I can, for example, point out that] 'When there is love, there is no jealousy, no hate,' and go into it, convey it, with my blood.

Commentator: Properly to meet problems related to questions about love, jealousy, and so on, is to see them, observerlessly and choicelessly, on the level of a truly meditative mind. Real love and compassion are there on the part of a teacher when his or hers is this state of mind, and, when these are there, a teacher will, as Krishnamurti suggests here, expend energy to point out to others in the classroom with her or him the truth of meditative mind awareness and matters related to it, that is, the understanding, intelligence, and meaningfulness of living which are possible when there is the meditative mind.

2.26

Krishnamurti: [As a teacher I can] talk about prejudices, what prejudices are, and so on ... go into it. [I can ask the students], "Can you be free, can you put away your prejudices, not for a time, but put them completely away?"

Commentator: A good example of how a teacher concerned about meditative mind awareness and about the unconditioning of the mind which is part of that awareness might proceed in a classroom is given in this statement. This is perhaps part of the talk involved in that ten or fifteen minute timespan Krishnamurti mentioned in an earlier quoted statement, when there is a coming off the "pedestal" on which the teacher operates in order to transmit to students left-brain intellectual or right-brain partially functioning mind related understandings. In this case, however, as Krishnamurti has made clear, the teacher's talk and questioning are not at all related to methods and to teaching and learning strategies which are properly there when the concern is teaching and learning on the level of a partially functioning mind, as in the case of teaching and learning of some academic subject.

2.27

Krishnamurti: The pedestal, [that is,] I am the teacher, you are the taught ... spoils relationship with my students.

Commentator: What is proper and applies to teaching and learning on the level of a partially functioning mind is not proper and appropriate as regards awakening of loving intelligence and understanding on the level of the meditative mind. This is at least part of what could be said to be the meaning of this statement by Krishnamurti. Teacher and student are necessarily apart, but not necessarily in the sense of in conflict or opposition, when there is the merely partially functioning mind teaching and learning which are of exclusive concern in much, if not all education today. When there is learning related to meditative mind awareness, the relationship as regards the teacher and the students in a particular classroom which must be there, Krishnamurti here indicates, is one where there is no separation between teacher and learners, that separation required when there is teaching and learning on the level of the merely partially functioning mind. When there is real learning related to awareness on the level of a truly quiet mind, each one in the classroom is both a teacher and a learner. This is to say that in this case the teacher and the learner are one and the same. All those in the classroom who are learning in relationship to living, to relating, are really together exploring, discovering, communicating.

2.28

Krishnamurti: [Once the teacher has shown the student something related to living, to relating, then she or he has] planted a seed. [Then the teacher can] push [the student] further.

Commentator: "Pushing" here, of course, is figurative. It would be wrong to think that it means unduly influencing, conditioning, coercing, compelling, and so on. If there is living truth, and, if it is possible for one to discover it and live in relationship to it, to the understanding of such truth and the loving intelligence related to it, one might well suggest that educators do well if they have a concern that students come to understand and live in accord with such truth. Planting "a seed" in this regard is what a teacher in a classroom does when he or she makes time to talk about and to describe the truly meditative mind, what it means in her or his own life, how it makes possible an other than ordinary, usual awareness, and so on. For such a teacher to return from time to time and again and again to further description of these sorts of things and to engage students in discussion of them are several ways in which the teacher can "push" the students further.

2.29

Krishnamurti: [When the teacher is not the authority, the one who knows, there is no reason for a] group, [a] following, [for the teacher being] caught in [his or her] own little capacity and in exaggerating that capacity and giving [herself or himself] self-importance, which means [the teacher] must take an interest in, or be responsible for, the whole thing.

Commentator: Though it might be said that a teacher has a responsibility related to the particular academic subject which she or he teaches, a responsibility related to that teacher's doing her or his utmost correctly or accurately to transmit aspects of some particular discipline, be it a science or one of the arts, to students, it could also be said that his or hers is shared responsibility for "the whole thing." The "whole thing" might be said to be totality of the mind, the mind which functions partially but which also is completely silent, meditative. The "whole thing" might also be said to be the living and not just the abstract, might be said to be all of awareness and not just rational, conscious awareness.

2.30

Krishnamurti: Have a relationship with ... students ... in which there is no motive ... no self-interest.

Commentator: Though a teacher is "on a pedestal" when there is teaching and learning of a particular subject in a classroom, he or she must come down off of it when there is teaching and learning related to meditative mind awareness and understanding, when she or he together with students "goes into" matters related to such awareness and understanding. When there is such "going into" or exploration of such matters, then there is no place for any motive related to partial functioning mind activity of some kind, that is, no place for self functioning, self thinking, planning, influencing, arguing, and so on. Such exploration implies, this is to say, total silence of the mind, mind which has stopped all of its partial functioning, all engagement in activity. As regards those in the classroom whose minds are in such a state of complete silence, for them there can be discovery of or learning about living or relating. For them, there can be real answers to questions about right living, right relationship, about meaning in living, about truth in living. For them, there can be real love, supreme intelligence, fullness of understanding, insight, and wisdom as well as living which is not fragmented but rather integral, fully human.

2.31

Krishnamurti: [When there is learning related to living or relating, then, strictly speaking, the teacher is] not teaching [the student, the student is] not teaching [the teacher, but rather,] together, [they] are going into [the matter] deeply.

Commentator: When there is a partially functioning mind focus of teachers and students on some particular academic subject or discipline in a classroom, then the teacher, as one already knowing the particular subject matter, as one having partially functioning mind related insight into some particular art form and perhaps considerable ability and skill related to it, is "on a pedestal." When, however, there is learning related to matters psychological, living, relating, then there is no pedestal, no teacher separate from the learner and no learner separate from the teacher. Then each one in the classroom is both teacher and learner. Everyone in the classroom, this is to say, can go into meditative mind awareness and into matters related to it, but, of course, it is possible that not all in the room will actually do so. Some may, and some may not, but for those who do, there can be deep understanding of living and living-related matters, theirs can be meditative mind awareness, understanding, and insight, loving intelligence and profound wisdom. For them, there can be a mind really transformed, totally revolutionized.

2.32

Krishnamurti: By talking [the teacher learns] from [himself or herself] as well as from the student.

Commentator: This is learning in the classroom, but it is not learning related to the structure and organization that must be there if there is to be mastery on the part of students of some particular subject matter, some particular academic discipline. This is saying that as regards living or relating, each one, student and teacher in a classroom, or anyone outside of it, can be both teacher and learner. The relationship, in this case, is not that of teacher and learners to some particular subject matter or academic discipline but rather to living, to its meaning and significance.

2.33

Krishnamurti: [The teacher] might help [the student] accelerate [her or his] own learning.

Commentator: This learning is learning about life, about right living, about the world as one goes along in life, moment to moment, day to day, which might be related to time spent in a classroom or related to one's being outside of it. Learning then is not theoretical, related to accumulations in a partially functioning mind. The learning then is not learning which is seeking, not learning with a motive on the part of the learner to know, to understand theories and concepts, to come to an appreciation of and/or to engage in the production of works of art, to engage in activities related to artistic endeavours, including literary ones. When there is learning which is search rather than seeking, then there is no motive, no self, and so deep understanding, full and complete, can come to the mind. Then there can be, this is to say, communion with what *is*, the living, the eternal, the unknowable. In educational settings, besides learning related to the theoretical, the abstract, related merely to left and right-brain partial mind functioning, it is possible that there be real, direct learning about life, about right relationships, about matters psychological. This would be education related to the awakening of meditative mind awareness and not just for left-brain rational and right-brain intuitive awareness on the level of the merely partially functioning mind. There is no place, however, when there is proper partial mind functioning, for any exaggerated, indeed false claims relative to what a partially functioning right-brain can do. Such claims, we have seen, are made, for example, by Stuart Parker and Tobin Hart, and, as we shall see later, by John L. Brown and Cerylle A. Moffett,[3] this when they suggest that partial right-brain mind functioning can capture something of the living whole, that it can commune with the timeless, that it can come upon that supreme intelligence and profound wisdom which are really there only when there is the state of the truly meditative mind.

2.34
Krishnamurti: [The] relationship between the educator and the educated should be non-authoritarian.
Commentator: On the level of the partially functioning mind there is one sense of authority that applies to the teacher of some particular academic discipline. The teacher can be expected to know the subject matter such that she or he can rightly transmit to students a correct understanding of it. Being able to do this means that she or he is an authority as regards the particular academic discipline taught. As regards those times when the teacher comes off the superficial level, steps down from the pedestal, it can be said that the teacher is no longer an authority for then there is no subject matter that he or she knows and relative to which the teacher can be an authority. Thus, in the exploration of meditative mind awareness each one, teacher and student, must be his or her own authority. This puts the teacher and the student on the same level when and as they explore and discover together what it is to live rightly, what it is rightly to relate to others, to the world, to the totality of what *is* and not just to some part of it.

2.35

Krishnamurti: Structure is a plan you make beforehand and try to adhere to; I do not want any structure in teaching.

Commentator: It is important that teaching and learning on the level of the partially functioning mind be structured, that lessons be planned, that learning strategies be employed by the teacher, that there be evaluation and testing of what is learned, and so on. When, however, teaching and learning are related to meditative mind awareness, then there is no place for structure, strategies, evaluation, and the like. Indeed, for a teacher to try to structure such teaching and learning would be to thwart, to work against discovery, on the part of herself or himself and on the part of students, of what, for example, is real love, total freedom of the unconditioned mind, supreme intelligence, awareness which is not consciousness, which is awareness utterly without self being there, and so on.

2.36

Krishnamurti: The moment [there] is a dialogue, there is separation between your brain and my brain. But when we are communicating together over something, we are both thinking about that, watching it. Therefore, we are in constant communication. We are both together, in exploring [the] fact, [for example], whether it is possible to be free or not.

Commentator: As it is now, dialogue is always, or most often in relation to partial functioning of the mind. This is to say that in its usual or currently ordinary sense dialogue implies division, separation as regards the thought and thinking of the participants in the dialogue. Each participant before, during, and after the dialoging continues to believe in and to adhere to his or her particular partially functioning mind derived conclusion, to her or his particular ideological stance, but, as a result of the dialoging, there is a greater measure of tolerance relative to those conclusions which are other than his or her own. However, in a classroom, on the part of the teacher and students exploring and discovering in relationship to a truly meditative mind, there must be no such division or separation. Rather, teacher and students must, as Krishnamurti says here, communicate "together over something." Their watching or observation of something must be observerless and choiceless if there is to be complete understanding of this something related to living, to discovery of something which has to do with real meaning in living.

2.37

Krishnamurti: [When, for example, the teacher and the student] are both investigating fear, not conclusions or anything else, [they] must establish communication. And communication ceases when there is a dialogue, or questioning. But when [they] are thinking, when [they] are concerned, about the same thing, then both of [them] are in communication, because [both] are looking at the same thing.

Commentator: When there is learning in relationship to the truly meditative mind, there is no teacher and those taught, as there is when there is partially functioning mind teaching and learning, as when, for example, the concern is the teaching and learning of some science. When appropriate, there can be movement beyond the level of the partially functioning mind, movement to the level of the deep, truly meditative mind, that level whereon there is no self at all, no self as teacher and no self as learner.

For there to be transcendence to the level of the truly meditative mind in a classroom in which partially functioning mind related academic subjects are taught and learned, there must be a leaving behind of the partially functioning mind and all of its products. When there is deep learning and "teaching" related to it, there is no teacher separate from learner as there is when there is partially functioning mind related teaching and learning.

2.38

Krishnamurti: The moment dialogue or discussion takes place, there is a breakage of communication. [It is important that teacher and students] be in communication in [direct] examination [of something, that they be in] communion [when they are] investigating [something] directly.

Commentator: What Krishnamurti is talking about here in the latter part of this statement is discovery or learning in relationship to meditative awareness and understanding of matters related to living. Dialogue or discussion as referred to in the first part of this statement usually or ordinarily means separation, give and take, as regards selves or partially functioning minds speaking out of particular ideological stances, political, religious, or otherwise, from a so-called personal perspective, in relation to some so-called personally held opinion or point of view. When the concern is matters of living or relating, then it is important for all in a classroom – teacher and students – together to examine, to investigate, to explore directly, without any opinion, belief, particular vision, and so on, interfering with the examination or investigation. Then the examination or investigation is not at all out of thinking on the level of a partially functioning mind, that level of the mind which is appropriate when the matter is some academic discipline. The examination or investigation then is out of that fullness of attention which is love, which is loving, rather than merely rational intelligence.

2.39

Krishnamurti: When we discuss, or have a dialogue, our minds are not in communication, because then you are thinking for yourself. Here both of us want to find out, go into it, explore the whole thing, so our brains are communicating with each other, so there is not me and you, battling about it.

Commentator: 'Communication,' as used in the first sentence of this statement relates to a truly meditative mind. It means communion of minds in a state of awareness which is not consciousness. To discuss, to dialogue, to debate something, or to argue in favor of some partially functioning mind derived conclusion is to be on the level of a partially functioning and not a fully functioning mind, to be on that level of the mind which implies or entails division or separation of minds, that is, "me" and "you." In education, what is needed is not only proper development of partially functioning minds but also concern for and a cultivation of fully functioning ones.

2.40

Krishnamurti: [When out of discussion] with ... students [there comes understanding of a problem related to living, then] the awakening of intelligence is action, [then] action and intelligence are not separate.

Commentator: When there is a partially functioning mind, there is a time interval between its partial intelligence, between the understanding which is related to this intelligence and any action which can and might follow in relationship to this understanding, for example, actualization of an ideal, the application of a concept, and so on. All of this is appropriate when the problem is a scientific or technological one, one related to some practical aspect of living, but not when the concern and matter is right living, is relating rightly. In relationship to the living what is appropriate is meditative mind awareness. When such awareness is there, comes to the mind, the intelligence which is also there is itself action, the only action which is needed in relation to the matter at hand, so to speak. This intelligence is loving rather than abstract or rational, and such intelligence is the answer to each and every problem of living or relating. Love is direct, immediate action, without that time interval which is there when there is partial intelligence and ensuing action on the level of a merely partially functioning mind. What is lacking in education today, on the part of teachers and students, is concern for and the direct action which is the loving intelligence of a truly meditative mind.

2.41
Krishnamurti: [There can be] conveying something ... to the student so that [both the teacher and the student] act instantly, see the right thing and do it, be finished with it.
Commentator: The "acting instantly" spoken about here is the action of love, of loving intelligence on the level of a truly meditative mind. It is this action alone which is the complete and adequate solution to each and every problem of living, of relating. When a teacher in a classroom "gets off" the superficial level of the mind – that level which is related to the pursuit of some particular academic discipline – he or she can convey to students the importance of such "getting off." When she or he does so, there is a concern that there be, particularly as regards students in the class, not only partially functioning minds but also ones which function fully.

2.42
Krishnamurti: [When there is investigating into oneself, but directly and] not theoretically, [there can be understanding related to living, relating rightly].
Commentator: Truly understanding the self is seeing the self for what it really is and does. It is to see that it is not anything real but merely something fashioned or made by a partially functioning mind. Truly to see this is to see out of an observerless, choiceless observation, with that fullness of attention which is there when there is a truly meditative, silent, quiet mind and not the one which relates to matters theoretical, namely, a partially functioning one. An education which is related to and in regard to which there is only concern for a partially functioning mind is a too limited education. Real revolution in education, that is truly significant change in education, is there when there is concern for and a "working" in relationship to the whole mind, mind which can function partially but which can also be silent, meditative.

2.43
Krishnamurti: Let us find out together how to clean the house, this house [which is the mind of the teacher or the mind of the student, so that there is complete freedom from] fear, [from] violence, not just a little bit but completely.
Commentator: The complete applies only to the totality of mind, silent as well as partially functioning. Partial mind functioning is necessary and appropriate as regards, for example, the doing of science, learning some skill or art, and so on. As regards living and problems of living what is appropriate is not a partially functioning mind but one which is truly

meditative. The loving intelligence of the truly silent mind can solve, so to speak, any problem of living or relating, be it fear, violence, or some other. "Cleaning the house" requires self-knowledge, that is meditative mind understanding of the self. Any education for the whole, for totality of mind functioning and living, gives proper place and time not only to the partial knowledge and understanding of academic subjects but also to meditative mind awareness and understanding of things related to it – freedom, love, wisdom, and so on.

2.44

Krishnamurti: When the student leaves [a school or a university] ... he [or she] must be completely changed. That is my concern. In that concern is my love; I love him [or her], so I am passionate about it.
Commentator: Complete, that is, radical, revolutionary change can be there in a student when he or she leaves a school or university if and when all who are in it have a concern for and expend energy in relation to a fostering of not only partially functioning minds but also of fully functioning, truly meditative ones. Any school or university which promotes development, so to speak, of meditative minds and not just partially functioning ones is radical and revolutionary as regards what goes on it. People in it are not only those who work for so-called educational change which is not fundamental change, and this because it involves mere movement from one point within consciousness to another and not that radical movement which is transcendence to awareness other than conscious awareness. It is only awareness which is not conscious awareness which relates to the new, the fresh, and the dynamic rather than to what is the old, the stale, and the static. It is awareness which is not conscious awareness which is there when there is communion with what *is*, the real rather than the merely ideal, the eternal rather than the merely temporal, which is there when there is living in relationship to such communion.

Such, then, is the "methodology" question and some answers to it. If someone were to raise the question of what justification on moral grounds there is or might be for a teacher to act or to proceed in accord with what this "methodology" suggests, a reply would be that justification properly relates to actions in accord with a partially functioning mind, but not to one which is functioning totally. If there is another level of the mind transcendent to the level of partial functioning, one cannot justify, in the usual way, by recourse to principles, to norms of morality in the usual sense, anything related to this level. One cannot use rational intelligence to justify loving intelligence, nor activity appropriate to the known to justify the action which is related to the unknown, the eternal, the immeasurable, namely, love. Similarly one cannot use the part to justify the whole nor the unreal, the ideal, the inert, or the abstract to justify the real, the dynamic, the living. What one can say is that love or the living whole is its own eternity and its own justification, and so one should not ask it to justify itself as one rightly does when actions have to do with matters merely but appropriately related to time, to a partially functioning mind. Just as one rightly does not, indeed cannot argue about living, so too one rightly does not, indeed cannot justify the living but rather only that which is on the level of thought. One does not, indeed cannot justify any action which is out of love, or rather that only real action which is the action of love. Furthermore, the morality of real love is always deep, not of the superficial level of mind which is requisite when there is need to justify action in relation to time, to a merely partially functioning mind.

When there is awareness of the real beyond the unreal, the unknown beyond the known, the living beyond the dead, and so on, then, one might say, on the part of those responsible for a school or a school system it is this awareness in and of itself which will be that which prompts them, and also those who work within such a school or school system, to work, so to speak, not only for the cultivation of properly partially functioning minds but for truly meditative ones as well.

In the next chapter, the concern is not the classroom and what is appropriate as regards what goes on in it relative to the cultivation of not only properly partially functioning minds but fully meditative ones as well. In the next chapter the concern is the whole school and the whole so-called school system, indeed the whole of the so-called educational "enterprise" and radical, revolutionary change in relation to it.

Chapter Three

Schools and the Meditative Mind

> Wisdom ... is [not] a thing to be learnt, to be accumulated .... If it is, then it becomes mere knowledge, a thing of experience and of the books .... Wisdom is ever new, ever fresh, and there is no means of gathering it.

> Our so-called education everywhere is ... teaching the young to conform, religiously, morally, economically .... But through right education we could perhaps bring about a different understanding by helping to free the mind from all conditioning – that is, by encouraging the young to be aware of the many influences which condition the mind and make it conform.

> J. Krishnamurti

Not only can it be said that there can and must be radical change in what goes on in classrooms if education is to have relevance not only to thought-related but also to living-related matters, if there is to be learning by teachers and students in classrooms not only in relationship to partially functioning minds but also to truly meditative ones, but schools and school systems, universities and colleges as a whole can be radically changed, with all who are in them, including administrators, not only concerned about such change but expending energy to bring about such change. In this chapter it is educational change beyond the classroom which is the matter for consideration. This consideration takes the form of commentary on excerpts from recently published books which deal with the question of educational change.

First, we listen to excerpts from *Beyond Modernism and Postmodernism: Essays on the Politics of Culture* by Maurice R. Berube, *Restructuring High Schools for Equity and Excellence: What Works* by Valerie E. Lee and Julia B. Smith, and *Redesigning School: Lessons for the 21ˢᵗ Century* by Joseph P. McDonald.[1] We can see that all that is said in these excerpts about the need for change in education is merely theory related, hence related merely to a partially functioning mind. When there is choiceless, observerless looking at education today, there is seeing of the need for radical, revolutionary change, which is not at all considered in these books. Such seeing, which is not the kind of seeing which relates to what is said in these books, is only possible when there is understanding that not all awareness is consciousness, that all of the mind is not merely partially functioning, that it can be completely silent, meditative. When it is so, it is not at all dead, but highly sensitive and deeply understanding.

All educational talk in education has been and is related to calls for reformation and not real revolution since it has always implied and still implies mere movement from one pattern of thinking to another, from the products of one part of a merely partially functioning mind to other products of the same part or of some other part of such a mind. Increasingly and specifically, one can see in education and elsewhere, as in psychology and religion, movement from left-brain products, that is, ideas and concepts, to right-brain products, namely, images and symbols, myths and stories. Often there are exaggerated, indeed false claims made with regard to this movement from idea and concept to story and myth, often referred to as a new appreciation of the so-called wisdom which is supposed somehow to enable one to understand and profit from so-called "lived experience." Experience and living, however, are two different things. The first is of the past, dead and gone, and the second is the dynamic, the ever-changing unknowable, to be communed with in the state of the truly meditative mind, but not measured, limited, captured in image or concept. One is in illusion if one thinks that reflecting on experience, one's own or that of others, brings one close to living, to an understanding of living.

3.0

Lee & Smith: Renewal activities, although they help existing organizations function more efficiently, do not really change what those organizations actually do. Reform activities reach somewhat deeper, in that they change existing procedures and rules in an organization in order to help it adapt to changing circumstances.

Commentator: There can be profound, deeply significant change which is not at all related to some concept or idea, which, if implemented, merely makes for reformation, for movement from one point within the whole of consciousness to another. Merely to engage in reform in education is not to address the question: how can there be real revolution in the mind such that there is learning on the part of teachers and students not only in relation to mastery of academic subjects or disciplines, and in relation to an appreciation and, for those with skill and ability, the production of works of art, but also the right living or relating which awareness on the level of the meditative mind makes possible? If and when many, if not all individuals, in the sense of those who are whole and undivided, relate rightly, then society, that is these same individuals, will be transformed, enlightened.

3.1

McDonald: What does the school believe? What knowledge does it cherish? In redesigning [itself], the school asks itself what it proposes to accomplish in the minds and hearts of the students it teaches .... The work always involves what is called vision.

Commentator: Given the fragmentation which is there in educational institutions today, one can say that the lack of the meditative mind awareness which can make for encompassing or enveloping order in living, in behaviour, as well as any efforts made merely to reform rather than revolutionize schools and universities will lead to continuing failure. As it is, actual functioning of schools and universities makes for mediocrity in that mind functioning in them is always and merely partial and never total, related always, this is to say, to fashioning of mind fragments like beliefs and visions and never to the total mind which, though it can function partially, can also be completely silent, truly meditative. So long as this state of affairs is not radically changed so that meditative mind awareness comes to the fore in schools and universities, there cannot be, so to speak, "better" schools. As it is, accomplishments "in the minds and hearts of students" might make for improved left and right-brain partial mind functioning but have nothing at all to do with minds which are truly meditative and therefore deeply understanding, with intelligence that is loving and not merely rational.

3.2

Berube: By the close of the twentieth century, intellectuals changed focus ... they became university academics with expertise in narrow disciplines. They introduced the academic discipline of "cultural studies."

Commentator: Education in some decades of the last century was a reflection of partial functioning mind movement away from what was considered to be overemphasis on left-brain to more of a right-brain emphasis. At other times the pendulum swung the other way again. Both types of movement, however, were merely within the whole of consciousness, hence did not at all relate to fullness of understanding which is possible when there is a fully functioning mind, meditative mind awareness. The 1990s emphasis on preparing students for efficient functioning in corporations and business or that on cultural studies was as fragmentary and limited as any other movement in a preceding decade. Only when there are schools and universities in which there is concern not only for the development of partially functioning minds but also for the total functioning of meditative minds can there be education for totality of learning and being, for fullness of living in relationship not only to time but also to the timeless, not only to thought-related concerns but directly to the real, what *is*, for real, loving relationships with everyone and everything, for the supreme intelligence, insight, and wisdom which are there only when the mind is profoundly meditative.

3.3

Berube: A new amorphous discipline has emerged in academia: cultural studies .... The cultural studies movement is a strong, programmatic attempt of universities to address, in a unified fashion, the problems of a global universe.

Commentator: This statement points to the narrowness of focus and fragmentation which are present in education today. In every field of academics, in, for example, feminine, minority, and cultural studies and the like, there is always and only movement of the mind within the whole field of consciousness, in relation to opposites, in reaction to some opposing stance. Those who, for example, see education as merely necessary preparation of an efficient workforce for big business and those who oppose what they consider to be such a narrow understanding of what education is or ought to be are simply moving in the hallway of opposites. Any standard of 'excellence' which is prized by either side of this opposition is narrow and limited, not at all related to that supreme intelligence which might be said to characterize a truly meditative mind, mind beyond all opposites, in communion with what really *is*, the whole, the living, the actual. When there is no wastage of energy by a partially functioning mind moving, often wrongly and futilely, within the field of consciousness, of opposites, then there is the energy to discover what *is* real, the living, the answer to each and every question related to what is right living, right relating.

3.4

McDonald: [In] the twenty-first century school ... values on the inside may be tuned to values on the outside. [One of the] key challenges of the tuning arena of school design [is] balancing intimate perspectives with critical ones.

Commentator: Beliefs, opinions, values, perspectives, and the like, all relate to a partially functioning mind. Any reform or change for the so-called better as regards beliefs or values, if this merely means dropping some beliefs or values and adopting others, or any casting aside of one perspective in order to embrace another, is not radical, revolutionary change. Rather than a merely partially functioning mind functioning in relation to some opposite like the internal or "inside" on the one hand, or the external or "outside" on the other, there can be a completely silent, fully understanding mind which functions partially only when necessary and appropriate. Then there can be left-brain or intellectual understanding of things solely related to time, that is, science, technology, and practical matters, as well as appropriate right-brain fashioning of images and symbols in relation to the arts, but otherwise, in relation to the timeless, the eternal, meditative mind awareness and understanding. If, in education, there is a concern for and real awakening of minds to the importance or significance of meditative mind awareness, then only can educational change be deep or profound.

3.5

Lee & Smith: How can schools change teachers' attitudes about their students' ability to learn and about the teachers' own abilities to be successful with all their students? We have no easy answer. Changing attitudes is not easily accomplished.

Commentator: Here, change is related only to a partially functioning mind. Unless there is radical, revolutionary change in education so that there is an awakening to the importance of meditative mind awareness, any change in attitude, in subject matter, in learning strategies, and so on, will be merely superficial. Any challenge made by a merely partially functioning mind so that there might be a giving up of some image of self, specifically that of the teacher or of the student, for some other image of self supposedly better than the one replaced is not an example of an expressed concern for the radical, revolutionary change which is needed in education today.

3.6

McDonald: Can we have schools at last that educate all children to use their minds well? ... People must first want such schools ... work very hard at getting them, and very patiently .... Finally, it will be necessary that we get clearer ... about the nature of the overall work of redesigning school .... This too will take much work and much patience.

Commentator: What societies and schools need is awakening to meditative mind awareness. With regard to education, what is needed is right pedagogy in relation to academic subjects so that there is rigor and rightness in teaching and learning related to them, but as well there is a need for seeing the limits of academic subjects, of academic disciplines, and of the mind which works in relation to them. What is needed also, however, is that which can give encompassing or enveloping shape to the whole of the educational enterprise, so to speak, thus helping to make possible holism in living or in relating on the part of individuals who are society, namely, meditative mind awareness and the supreme intelligence, fullness of understanding, and profound wisdom which are integral to such awareness.

3.7

Berube: We owe our students the most broadening intellectual experience possible. The search for knowledge ... imparts to students the importance of developing the human intellect to its outermost limits.

Commentator: Experiences relate to what is dead and gone, and not at all to what is new, the dynamic, that which is living. Communion with the living is possible only when the totality of the mind is not reduced to mere intellect, however necessary and worthwhile is a properly developed intellect. Rather than, as is suggested here, teachers expending or wasting energy dwelling in or exclusively focusing on the past, and thus not deeply or profoundly understanding anything, it is possible for them to come to the understanding of what the totality of the mind is and of its relation both to time and to the timeless. Theirs can be the understanding that, though their activities in relation to the discipline they teach and in relation to their conveying to students the importance of the development of intellect are merely related to partial functioning of the mind, and, though it is important for them to do their utmost to initiate students into a proper understanding of this discipline, theirs also is a responsibility to spend time exploring with students the matter of meditative mind awareness and all that such awareness makes possible.

In the excerpts which follow now, several by Nel Noddings who introduces *School Leadership – Balancing Power with Caring,*[2] and some by Kathleen Sernak, its author, we see confusion of things related to two different levels of the mind. 'Power' relates to a merely partially functioning mind, and, when its limits are not properly understood, its exercise can easily become problematic. Real, deep 'caring' is not of a partially functioning but of a truly meditative mind, that level of mind whereon there is no self, hence no motive, no design, and so on, what is there when there is exercise of power, whether proper or improper. To mix these two levels of the mind, and to mix up power and caring is to mix the known or what is of the known with the unknowable, what is of time with the timeless. The result of any such mixing or mixing up can only be confusion and conflict.

3.8

Noddings: Care theory ... emphasize[s] caring as a relation, [that is] one in which the carer attends ... to the needs of the cared-for, and the cared-for ... acknowledges ... the care [given].

Commentator: The caring relation described here is not real for it involves separation of the carer from the cared-for. Self is there caring, and another self is there being cared for. Self is not anything real, however, and so actually what there is here is one image relating to another image. All merely image relationships are superficial, merely involving activity on the level of a partially functioning mind, not at all out of love, not at all related to the action of a mind which is truly loving and whose intelligence is loving. What would make for deep, profound change in education is not a mixing up of matters related to real caring with those which are related to the exercise of power, but real caring on the part of all within a school or university as well as a limiting of the exercise of power always to the barest necessity, indeed an avoidance of its use whenever possible.

3.9

Noddings: A principal must ... use his or her power to build structures and institute procedures that will support caring throughout the web of care. [Many] leaders, [that is principals,] argue that they are enacting unpopular measures because they "care."

Commentator: If a principal's mind is truly meditative, then real caring will be there, and there will be required partial functioning of the mind on his or her part, but only when this is necessary. It is not that there will be "caring power" for care is one thing and power another, each related to a different level of the mind, the first, if real, related to a truly meditative mind and there without "self" so-called caring, the second to a partially functioning mind. Rather, there will be caring on the level of the meditative mind, there all the time, and exercise of power in a sane, rational, but limited way but only when this is necessary or appropriate. If self is there so-called caring, this self will likely engage in activity of some kind, to impose its own will on others, to condition minds or other selves with its own visions, wishes, desires, and so on, with in a word, some or all of its own limitations. To talk about "caring power" is to confuse time and the timeless, the known and the unknown, the dead and the living, the measurable and the immeasurable. Confusion always means lack of understanding, and, when there is lack of understanding, there is conflict and confusion in living, in relating, in behaviour.

3.10

Sernak: The total narrative [presented in this book] embodies not only an intellectual and academic description and interpretation of the data, but also a reflection of the conflicts and tensions I experience as a "caring person" .... Although much has been written about the particular concepts of caring and power, few theorists have written about the integration and linkage between caring and power.

Commentator: This statement talks about self or person as if it were something real. Whether so-called caring or not, self or person is merely a fashioning by a partially functioning mind. Indeed, when self is there, it can be the cause of conflict, as well as of confusion. It is confusion which is there when there is effort on the part of a merely partially functioning mind attempting to integrate and link caring and power. Clarity, rather than confusion of mind, as well as fullness of understanding are there when one sees that caring is of a truly meditative mind and power of a partially functioning one, and that unduly to mix the two is a recipe for confused thinking and for conflict in behaviour related to such thinking.

3.11

Sernak: Efficiencies, rights, individualism, abstraction, and generalities ground the current bureaucratic hierarchy of schools ... caring, most often conceptualized in terms of the individual, must be reconceptualized from the perspective of caring for and about the whole ... I [suggest] that attempts to create an ethic of caring within bureaucratic organizations become a politics of caring, an integration of caring and power.

Commentator: The "whole" here is not the living, the eternally alive. Real caring relates to mind in communion with what *is*, the eternally living, and not to some ethic(s) created by a partially functioning mind, the primary focus of which is the ideal rather than the real, what *is*, which deals in oughts and shoulds, hence relates to what *is* indirectly rather than directly and immediately as does a truly meditative mind. The time interval which is there between a partially functioning mind's formulated principles and their application is not there in the case of the truly meditative mind, and so its action, the action which is love, complete attention and fullness of intelligence, is immediate, is action now in relation to what *is* now.

Power, which is totally related to a partially functioning mind, is to be limited as much as possible and exercised only when necessary. Caring, on the other hand, if real, is there always in the state of the meditative mind. The "whole" in this statement is merely the collective, the institution, the organization, the community standing opposite to the individual. Merely to shift so-called caring which implies self there caring and thus not really caring, from the individual to the so-called "whole" is merely to move in the hall of opposites. When opposites are there, the awareness which is there is merely conscious awareness, and mind merely in a state of partial functioning, and thus there cannot be depth of insight, of understanding, possible only when there is the state of the truly meditative mind. Education truly revolutionized is education in relation not just to a merely partially functioning mind but significantly or importantly to the truly meditative mind.

3.12
Sernak:　　　　Relationships are essential to living fully as a human being and to developing viable communities.

Commentator:　　Relationships which are there when self, that is, a partially functioning mind is there are not and cannot be related to fullness of living. This is so whether such a mind is that of one who stands apart from others, apart from a community whose minds are also functioning partially, or whether it functions in consort with the community, in so-called harmony with the collectivity, that is, other partially functioning minds. Partial functioning of the mind is always and necessarily fragmentary and superficial. Human beings who are living fully have minds which function partially when such functioning is necessary and appropriate, but which are otherwise completely silent, hence functioning totally in that the functioning is action-related and not merely activity-related as is the case when the mind functions partially. This is to say that the totality of one's humanity has to do not only with thinking, proper partial left and right-brain functioning, but also with living, with loving. Education related to concern for and an expending of energy so that minds are in a truly meditative state as well as functioning partially when this is necessary is education related to human beings living fully.

3.13
Sernak:　　　　To be able to care is to know oneself, to understand where oneself begins and ends .... Understanding of self is necessary for

a principal in order to lead staff to reflect on not only their individual selves, but their collective selves, and how the latter affect the goals, organization, and interactions within the school.

Commentator: An individual self stands opposite to a collective self, and both are mere fashionings out of thought, out of a merely partially functioning mind. Both are situated within consciousness. There is an end to both of these selves when there is transcendence beyond all consciousness such that there is awareness which is not consciousness, that is, awareness in the state of the truly meditative mind. To understand all of this is to be self-knowing, to know the self, what it is and what it does, often creating confusion and conflict within and outside of educational institutions, as when it is there to "affect the goals, organization, and interactions within the school." Rather than staying always and ever on the superficial level of the mind, that level of the mind which entails self or selves being there, principals in schools and others in education can see, choicelessly and observerlessly that, though the mind can function partially, and that at times it must do so, it can be completely silent, in communion with the real, the living. With the understanding which comes of such seeing, such attention, there can be schooling revolutionized, that is, schooling not just to develop proper partially functioning minds but so that the learning of teachers and students, indeed of all within the school or university, including principals and other administrators, is related not just to mastery of academic subjects or disciplines, and to activities related to such mastery, but in relation to living, to relating rightly to everyone and everything.

3.14

Sernak: An ethic of caring as the basis for schooling will require providing opportunities for staff members to connect with themselves and to see themselves as separate from each other and from their students. Only when they are able to see the students as different from themselves, can they begin to care.

Commentator: When one talks about "connecting with oneself," one's talk reflects belief that the self, sometimes called inner or deeper, is something real. This statement suggests that the teacher's "self" can connect and separate, and so it can, but, if the self is not real, and indeed it never is, then its connecting and separating are not at all related to real relationships but rather to merely image ones, that is, merely thought or partially functioning mind created ones. When partial functioning of the mind is necessary, then there is separation of observer from the observed and separation of the thinker from the thought, but such separation cannot be there if there is real caring. Only when students and teachers are on the same level, with no separation between them, can theirs be real communication, that is, communion.

3.15
Sernak: An ethic of caring, implemented for political purposes, may be used to further self-interest under the guise of creating community when, in fact, it becomes a means for furthering one's own interests and ideologies.
Commentator: Real caring is not related to any ethic(s), to any morality created by a partially functioning mind. Caring is one thing and politics another. The first, if real, is meditative mind related, and the second partially functioning mind related. Real caring is not there, either, if community is merely a collectivity of partially functioning minds, minds which, just because they are merely and always partially functioning, are related to the particular group's own interests, or to some particular individual's, for example, the so-called community leader's, self-interest. Communities are often ideologically based and greatly concerned about communicating and promoting their own particular ideological beliefs. Unduly mixing up caring and politics can only lead to confusion within educational settings and elsewhere.

3.16
Sernak: School organizational patterns founded on a hierarchy of leadership are counterproductive to caring.
Commentator: If there is clear understanding that leadership and caring are not related, in that the first has to do with a partially functioning mind and the latter with a truly meditative mind, then leadership is limited, properly hedged in so that in an educational setting, for example, a school principal does not seek unduly to control teachers and students in order to impose his own ideas, to advance his own ambitions, and so on, so that he or she does nothing to hamper the exploration and discovery, by teachers and students, of matters having to do with living or relating. Then her or his leadership will be merely administrative and function-related, without status, and it will not be, so to speak, "counterproductive to caring." Strictly speaking, of course, for something to be counterproductive to something else, both must be on the same level, the level of opposites, both having to do with a superficially, partially functioning mind, with things related to this level of the mind.

3.17

Sernak: If schools are to be caring places ... the concept of leadership needs to be re-examined and the role of "leader," perhaps, redefined.

Commentator: Whether one is in a school or outside of it, when one's mind is in a meditative state, one is caring. Such a state of mind can always be there even when partial functioning of the mind is useful or necessary. If this one is a principal in a school, leadership will be exercised appropriately, but limited to matters which are properly amenable to organization or administration. There will not be any attempt to exercise leadership in areas where there can be no leader, no psychological or spiritual authority, namely, matters related to awareness which is not consciousness, to a truly meditative mind, like love, caring, compassion, total freedom, complete order, and so on, and matters related to the exploration and discovery, on the part of teachers and students, of such things.

3.18

Sernak: If we can accept that both caring and power are relational, reciprocal, contextual, and socially constructed, we come closer to realizing a link between them. That realization acts to dispel the notion that they are dichotomous and posits instead the concept of "caring power."

Commentator: Power and caring are not at all related to one another. Power has to do with partial and caring with full functioning of the mind. This means that they are not reciprocal. Reciprocity of two things is possible only when they are on the same level, the level of opposites, the level where efforts might be made to overcome the opposition of the one to the other. Though power might be said to be contextual, real caring is not. When there is the state of the truly meditative mind, caring is without limits, without measure, not at all dependent on circumstances or context but rather ever-abiding. Also, though power is socially constructed, real caring is not.

Given all of this understanding, one can say that it is clear that there is no link between power and caring. Though they indeed are not to be thought of as dichotomous, this is not because of what is being suggested here but because they are not both of the level of the partially functioning mind, that level where opposites prevail, but rather power is of this level and caring is not. Anyone in a school setting who attempts to exercise "caring power" is engaged in activity related to confusion, a lack of real insight and understanding.

The creation spoken about in the next set of excerpts from Douglas J. Fiore's, *Creating Connections for Better Schools*,[3] we shall see, is not real creation for it relates to mere activity on the level of a partially functioning mind and not to the profound understanding of what creation really is when there is a mind in a truly meditative state.

3.19
Fiore: When students are able to find the caring, safety, security, and compassion they deserve, then our schools will have created a culture in which learning will flower endlessly.

Commentator: Physically speaking, safety and security in schools are important and effected by measures related to proper partial mind functioning. Caring and compassion, if real, however, are matters of meditative mind awareness. It is confusion or a lack of understanding which is there when there is a mixing up of these two levels of the mind, of matters which are merely time-related and those which are related to the living, the eternally alive and dynamic. Proper education is education related to depth of understanding and living truth. Educators who are properly aware of time and the timeless, and who also understand that the timeless is there only when there is an ending to time and to everything which is time-related, do not unduly confuse the physical and the psychological, and so they do not strive to condition the minds of students with any so-called psychological security when there is no basis for it, no basis in relation to actual living or relating. Fear, in relationship to the psychological, which is partially functioning mind fashioned, relates to what is there because that same merely partially functioning mind imagines, wrongly, that psychological security in relation to a mind which is merely functioning partially is a possibility when in fact there is not and cannot be any such security.

3.20
Fiore: This book comes at a time when the shouts and cries for school improvements and reforms are almost deafening. It comes at a time when many people believe that the answers we all seek for educational improvement, in all of its forms, lie in standards and accountability. I offer a different perspective.

Commentator: Perspective is related to observation out of a partially functioning mind, and any change in perspective can lead at best to mere reformation and never to revolution, that is, deep, profoundly significant change. What is needed in education is not mere reform but profound change related to awareness which is other than consciousness, that is, meditative mind awareness, and the action which is related to such awareness.

3.21

Fiore:　　　It is unreasonable ... to expect people to flourish in a culture that is disconnected and mired in negativity.

I hope this book helps you understand the power of a positive school culture.

Commentator:　　Negation related to meditative mind awareness is not at all related to the negativity which is mentioned here nor to any positivity which is opposed to it. Self is there whenever there are opposites, for example, a so-called loving self opposite to a hating self, a so-called connected self opposite to a so-called disconnected one, self moving in a self-created so-called positive culture opposite to an equally self-created negative culture. Only when there is no self there at all, psychologically speaking, can there be living in relationship to full flowering of intelligence and the action which is there when there is this intelligence. Only when, in schools, there is not just concern for a working towards the development of correctly and appropriately partially functioning minds but also concern for and time given for teachers and students to learn the significance of a truly meditative mind and all that meditative mind awareness makes possible will there be education revolutionized rather than merely reformed, and reformed because there is a more positive school culture in place, rather than one "mired in negativity."

3.22

Fiore:　　　We can continue to improve our schools. We will do it more readily when we create, foster, and sustain positive cultures as the foundation of positive school experiences for students.

Commentator:　　Learning from experience is possible and appropriate when the matter is temporal and physical, as in science and technology, and in relation to the practicalities of living, but not when the matter is psychological, related to actual living or relating. In these latter cases, what is possible and appropriate is learning as related to a meditative state of awareness. Then, there is not learning from experience, the dead and gone, whether the experience is that of the teacher, the student, or someone else, be that someone a so-called "wise person," a mystic, or a guru. This learning is necessarily moment to moment, is learning as one goes along in life and not at all related to accumulations in either a left or a right-brain partially functioning mind – ideas or concepts, images or symbols, stories or myths. It is not a revolutionized school which merely creates, fosters, and sustains a so-called positive culture, and in which the concern and energy expended is for merely correctly and appropriately partially functioning minds. Unless there is concern for and time given to awareness on the level of a truly meditative mind, schools can only continue to be mediocre. Such mediocrity is there even in those schools which might be said to be better than others as regards the development of properly partially functioning minds.

3.23

Fiore: School culture is the system of beliefs, values, norms, and expectations that governs the feelings and subsequent behaviors of all school constituents .... Depending on a variety of factors, school cultures can become positive, negative, or something in-between .... Schools with positive cultures experience greater levels of staff contentment and morale, many positive comments ... a sense of collegiality ... and an increase in student achievement, both formally measured, and informally observed. These schools are powerful institutions that radiate a positive sense of purpose.

Commentator: Cultures, in schools and elsewhere, are produced by partially functioning minds, as are the "beliefs, values, norms, and expectations" mentioned here. It is limited, superficial minds which would only and ever feel and behave out of the system made up of these fashionings of a partially functioning mind. So-called "powerful" schools, such as those characterized here, must be said, ultimately, to be mediocre in kind for the concerns and efforts of those in them relate only to fostering an ordinary or usual level of intelligence and understanding. Their so-called "sense of purpose" is related only to the shallow, the superficial. There is no concern for that depth of insight or understanding which is possible in the state of the truly meditative mind. Schools in which there is not only concern for and an expending of energy so that students might acquire expertise in areas which by their very nature demand partial functioning of the mind, but also so that theirs be minds which are truly meditative, hence deeply wise and understanding, lovingly intelligent, pefectly ordered, and completely insightful, are schools which relate to profound meaning and purpose in living.

3.24

Fiore: If we as educators continue to focus on "reforms of the day" without examining the supporting structure of our school culture, we are doomed for another era of trial and error.

Commentator: Merely to shift the focus of a partially functioning mind from one set of reforms judged to be inadequate to another set which, because its reforms rest on what is thought to be a better foundation, is merely to stay within the whole field of consciousness, to continue to remain only and always on the level of the necessarily limited partially functioning mind. To expect fullness of insight and understanding of a mind which is always functioning partially is unrealistic. Only a truly meditative mind is mind revolutionized and not merely related to what is reformed. Schooling reformed, like anything which is merely reformed, still has the old in it. Only when there is mind revolutionized can there be the new, the uncontaminated, the living rather than the dead and what is of the house of the dead. Schools and universities revolutionized and not merely reformed is what would constitute real, deeply significant change in education today.

3.25

Fiore: Never forget that our students deserve the best schools we can give them. Too many of them are wallowing in schools with negative cultures. These negative cultures have made too many students feel disconnected. Together, we can reconnect and turn these students back toward learning.

Commentator: Indeed, it is important that schools give students "the best" if "the best" includes understanding, on the level of a partially functioning mind, of mathematics, the sciences, the arts, practical living matters, and so on, but also, importantly, deep understanding on the level of the meditative mind of matters psychological, of right living, relating, behaving. "Disconnecting" and "reconnecting" imply belief in the reality of self. For schools, that is, teachers in schools to continue talking about and conditioning student minds with belief in self – lower or higher – as something real is not to promote "the best" for students. Rather, it is to create or to pass on to students what is illusion. If there is learning related not only to understanding on the level of a partially functioning mind but also learning, by teachers and students, in relation to a truly meditative mind, then schools have to do with minds truly revolutionized and not merely reformed.

3.26

Fiore: It is through school culture that we proclaim what we believe in and what goals we have for our students.

Commentator: Teachers proclaiming to students what they and others believe in or what they set or share as goals for students constitutes attempts to condition minds, and such activity cannot be justified by a properly and appropriately partially functioning mind. Neither would one whose mind is truly meditative say that such activity is appropriate. What is appropriate in schooling is allotting time for the development of proper partial functioning of the mind as regards time-related subjects and matters and, as well, giving due time for teachers and students in classrooms or halls of learning to learn, to explore, and to discover matters which have to do with right living, right relating, namely, supreme, loving intelligence and fullness of meditative mind understanding and insight.

3.27

Fiore: By dealing with all ... constituent groups and recognizing their contributions to school culture, we really can deal with individual needs in a collective manner .... This ... allows us and propels us to create a collective set of beliefs and a collective vision for our school. Such beliefs and vision become the foundation for a culture's growth .... This culture, as we now recognize, must be sustained over time so that the behaviors associated with it become automatic and habitual.

Commentator: Here, the "individual" and the "collective" are opposites, and, in schools and universities, to limit the mind merely to dealing in opposites is unduly to narrow down what is possible in education. To seek to initiate students into some particular "set of beliefs" such that their behaviour becomes "automatic and habitual" is a reflection of engagement in activity on the part of teachers which cannot be justified on the level of proper partial functioning of the mind, nor would one whose mind is truly meditative say that this is a proper thing for teachers to strive to do. So-called "collective vision" is merely projection out of inappropriately partially functioning minds. To seek to initiate students into a sharing in this vision is to seek to initiate them into shared illusion. As regards beliefs, what teachers and students can learn in relation to true meditative mind awareness is that there is no place for belief of any kind as regards right living, right relating, that any such belief militates against real communication, communion with the living which is possible only when there is mind beyond all beliefs. As regards living, beliefs are necessarily divisive and so to be totally negated by a fully functioning, completely understanding mind. As regards vision, what students and teachers can discover on the level of meditative mind awareness is that, as regards living or relating, vision always relates to the unreal, the ought, the should, but not at all to what *is*. Only a mind in communion with what *is* fully understands matters related to right living, right relating.

3.28

Fiore: When education becomes "stuck" or mired in techniques and beliefs that are reflective of the past is when it comes under the sharpest criticism.

Commentator: Any present related beliefs, perhaps called relevant to present day needs and concerns, are fundamentally no different from those which are said to reflect the past. As regards living or relating, any beliefs create division and conflict, and so proper education does not involve conditioning of minds with psychological and/or so-called spiritual beliefs. Techniques have no place either as regards matters of right living, right relationships. Rational beliefs, like sound, reasoned opinions have a place as regards matters physical and temporal, hence as regards the advancement of science and the betterment of technology, and so, in education there must be efforts expended by teachers and students for proper understanding of science and technology, for preparation of those who will work for further advancement of science and technology. Such beliefs and such opinions, however, have very little, if any value as regards matters related to living. Regarding such matters, what is needed and of value is meditative mind awareness and the intelligence and understanding related to it. Proper education includes concern and a making of time for teachers and students to explore and discover, so to speak, the treasures of meditative mind awareness.

3.29
Fiore: Throughout this book ... you have been required to take my words and the images they have created and see them come alive with your own eyes. That continues to be the real challenge.

I hope you will use your eyes and transfer the visions our students need to those you work with in the schools.
Commentator: To speak about words and images as coming alive is to confuse mere description of what is living with what is described, that is, actual living. Living is one thing, and words and images another. The "eyes" referred to here see illusion, the false, but not as illusion, as the false when, psychologically speaking, they see visions. Visions always relate to what is unreal, what is merely imagined, what is perhaps merely wished for, longed for. Teachers or educators who in relationship to living, to behaving, use partially functioning minds to create visions rather than dealing with what *is* are engaging in activity which is related to what is false, what is illusion. They also do what is improper when they strive to condition the minds of students with any such visions.

The next set of excerpts are from *Rethinking Educational Change with Heart and Mind*, edited by Andy Hargreaves, and with a foreword by Frances Faircloth Jones.[4] Merely to rethink educational change in relation to so-called heart and mind is to consider the question of needed change in education on the level of the merely partially functioning mind. Beyond mind and heart, beyond left and right-brain partial mind functioning, is the truly meditative mind, and, unless there is consideration of this question in relation to the deep level of the mind, there can only be answers which are partial and limited, indeed superficial.

3.30
Faircloth Jones: The engagement of the heart and being hopeful are routes to success in education.
Commentator: Here, heart is merely the opposite of intellect, of a rationally functioning mind. Hope is merely the opposite of despair. For those in education to stay always and only on the level of a mind which deals in opposites is unduly to limit education. Proper partial functioning of the mind is important, and teachers in the sciences and the arts act appropriately when they work to initiate students into a proper understanding of some particular academic discipline, be it a science or an art, and for application of such understanding. They do not really teach, however, if, in psychology, sociology, or education classes they proceed in accord with, for example, what is said by so-called transpersonal psychologists when they in effect suggest that less left and more right-brain partial mind functioning, or some synthesis of these two forms of a partially functioning mind, can make for depth of understanding and deeply meaningful living.

3.31
Hargreaves: Changes [in education] have been informed by better knowledge about successful approaches to teaching and learning.
Commentator: Real educational change is not merely reformatory but revolutionary, and revolution in education means awareness of and a working for not just proper partial functioning of the mind and the things which such functioning makes possible, but for meditative mind awareness and what it makes possible, namely, fullness of understanding and living, right relationship to everyone and everything, supreme, loving intelligence, profundity of wisdom, limitless mind order in relation not only to time but to the timeless, the eternally living, and communion with what really *is* rather than indulgence in illusion, that is, in inappropriate fashionings of a merely partially functioning mind.

3.32
Hargreaves: Efforts [to change education] have not gotten to the heart of what a great deal of teaching is about ... forming relationships with students, making classrooms into places of excitement and wonder, ensuring that all students are included and no one feels an outcast.

Commentator: If so-called teaching is merely functioning mind related, then the bonds and relationships effected by such functioning are merely of an image kind and not real for they involve selves, things ultimately unreal, so-called connecting with other selves equally unreal. Only when selves are not there at all are there truly meditative minds, and only when minds are truly meditative can there be that communion which makes for real relationships rather than merely image ones. When, as teacher and students together are learning about meditative mind awareness, there is communion, this communion means there are no selves there to feel included or excluded, to feel excited or bored. Theirs, then, is exploration and discovery of the nature and importance of supreme intelligence and deep understanding.

3.33

Hargreaves: [Preoccupation] with standards, targets, checklists, and form-filling can leave teachers with no time to care for or connect with their students ... with catastrophic results for their commitment and effectiveness.

Commentator: Ordinarily speaking, a teacher is one whose mind partially functions, is a self that knows some particular subject matter, and is one who is separate from the students, that is, those other selves who are the taught. Usually, students are those whose minds also function partially, are those who initially do not know the particular subject matter but are rather in the process of coming to know it. Though there can be caring, communion with the real or the living when the teacher's is meditative mind awareness, this caring or communion does not enter directly into the actual process of teaching and learning of particular subject matter. It comes into play, rather, when the teacher "comes off the superficial level," as Krishnamurti would say, when he or she puts subject matter concerns aside so as to explore and discover, with students, matters related to living, having to do with the eternal rather than the merely temporal. Though a teacher's commitment to initiating students into a proper and thorough understanding of the particular subject hers or his is a responsibility to transmit, which transmission he or she diligently strives to effect so that students indeed learn it, this is matter related to partial functioning of the mind and not to the total mind functioning which is meditative mind awareness and understanding. It is only when there is such awareness and understanding that real care and real relationships are possible. Without such awareness and understanding there can only be self or selves caring and relationships which are merely image-related and not reality-related.

3.34
Hargreaves: Emotions ... are ... an essential part of reason itself. If you cannot feel, you cannot judge ... teachers' emotional relationships with their students [are important]. Emotional intelligence [is] a central aspect of learning.
Commentator: To say that feelings are properly involved when there is sound judgment making is unduly to confuse left and right-brain partial functioning of the mind. To mix feeling in with judgment-making is to create confusion rather than any proper synthesis of left and right-brain partial mind functioning. So-called emotional relationships are never real relationships but rather merely right-brain related image ones. As such, they are necessarily limited and, because they are limited, they can be the cause of conflict and confusion in living. Then, there is neither the objectivity of a left-brain partially functioning mind nor proper functioning of the right hemisphere of the brain. Furthermore, the so-called "emotional intelligence" which is here claimed – but questionably so – to be an essential part of any learning on the level of a partially functioning mind is not the supreme, loving intelligence of mind in a truly meditative state, that state to which real depth of feeling and understanding relate. Merely intellectual understanding and emotions felt when mind is merely functioning partially have nothing at all to do with the state of the truly meditative mind. Proper education is related to the development of properly partially functioning minds but also to engagement in real, true meditative mind awareness.

3.35
Hargreaves: Teachers and schools [should be] developers of emotional intelligence [and hopeful. In face of] nakedly ideological reforms, [teachers'] identities ... purposes, [and] hope [are] vulnerable .... Without hope, there is no commitment, no optimism, no sense that children's lives can be made better. [It is important that] educators ... rekindle their hopes.
Commentator: If Andy Hargreaves were to say that writers in education like Stuart Parker and Tobin Hart who very much prize right-brain partial mind functioning are good examples of "developers" of "emotional intelligence," then, given what was said earlier about such advocates for greater right and less left-brain partial functioning of the mind in education, it can be said that there is no place at all to be made in education for this so-called "emotional intelligence." Any "educational change" along lines such as these would not at all be change for the better. Here too, in this statement's expressed criticism of "ideological reforms" and defense of so-called teachers' "identities," which are, but seemingly

not here understood to be, mere fashionings of a partially functioning mind, there is indicated prizing of right rather than left-brain partial mind functioning. Optimism is merely the opposite of pessimism or cynicism, and hope merely the opposite of despair. To move always and only in the tunnel of opposites is never to understand fully and deeply but always superficially. Any reforms in education advocated by minds moving always and only in this tunnel cannot bring about the change in education which makes for minds revolutionized, that is, minds which are not only properly partially functioning but also meditative when the matter is psychological, having to do with living, with relating rightly.

Rather than what is suggested relative to needed educational change in the following excerpts from *The Hero's Journey: How Educators Can Transform Schools and Improve Learning*, by John L. Brown and Cerylle A. Moffett,[5] it can be said that what are really needed in schools and universities are not heroes and heroines, that is, selves who have so-called developed or fulfilled themselves or who are on the way to the possession of so-called fully developed, fulfilled selves, who feel called to condition minds with their own idiosyncratic visions and dreams, things totally unrelated to what *is*, the actual, the living. What is needed, both within and outside of such places, are partially functioning minds functioning correctly and appropriately but also minds which are really meditative.

3.36

Brown & Moffett: The complexity of the current educational reform agenda demands courageous, responsible, determined action on the part of all .... To enact change ... we need bold action.

Commentator: Unless there is change related to revolution in the mind rather than the change which is mere reform effected by so-called "courageous, responsible, determined ... bold action" on the part of merely partially functioning minds, changes will not be profound and radical. They will rather merely relate to thinking and movement totally within the field of consciousness, to the neglect of awareness which is not consciousness, relate to mere partial rather than total functioning of the mind, that functioning which makes for depth of understanding, fully human right living or relating, supreme intelligence and profound wisdom, mind in perfect order, in joyful communion with what *is*, the eternally living.

3.37

Brown & Moffett: The call is to create schools capable of nurturing the intellectual potential, igniting the imagination, and developing the character of each and every student.

Commentator: Schools have a responsibility to strive to develop students' partially functioning minds, to nuture their "intellectual potential." Schools also act responsibly when they ignite the imagination of students relative to the creation of works of art, dramatic productions, and the like, but not when they encourage students to imagine and envision as regards psychological matters, in relation to right living, right relating, when they encourage students to read and study myths and legends in such a way as to suggest that these have to do with living wisely and with great intelligence and understanding. So to encourage the mind is to deal with what is unreal, what might be wished and longed for, what might be or ought to be, with what in a word is illusion rather than with what *is* and an ending of what *is* when this what *is* prevents or militates against living fully and in relation to deep meaning and purpose in living.

If the development of character is merely the building up of strong-willed individuals, that is willful selves whose minds are always functioning partially, then this does not at all relate to the right behaviour which meditative mind awareness makes possible. If, as a result of so-called development of character in schools, students merely live in relation to some merely partially functioning mind created ethics and morality, then their living is not at all related to the deeply moral living which is possible when minds are truly meditative.

3.38

Brown & Moffett: This ... book ... is an affirmation of the power and courage of shared vision, purpose, and inquiry.

Commentator: Power and courage are merely so-called virtues of a merely partially functioning mind and have nothing at all to do with a truly virtuous meditative mind. Vision is related to the unreal, and thus to share vision is to share what is not real, hence what is illusion. If this is indeed the case, any educational endeavours supposedly related to living or relating rightly but which really involve a sharing of vision(s) are futile activity. For those in education to proceed along these lines is for them to proceed without any depth of insight and understanding as regards what they are doing. If education is merely related to what merely partially functioning minds determine to be its proper purpose, then such education is narrow and limited, and it does not have anything to do with the depth of insight and understanding which are possible when there is a truly meditative mind. It is also very limited education which is there if inquiry is merely and always partially functioning mind related, if there is never time given for exploration and discovery in relation to truly meditative mind awareness and to the things which properly have to do with such awareness.

3.39

Brown & Moffett: In the collective wisdom of myth and legend we can find the inspiration for a heroic journey that is the destiny of all individuals and groups working today to transform schools into authentic learning organizations.

Commentator: There is no profound wisdom in any myth or legend. The journeying of any hero or heroine is journeying of a self, and, so long as self is there, there cannot be profound transformation in schools or elsewhere for real transformation is revolution in the mind such that there is selfless meditative mind awareness and not merely and always a self, even if called higher or deeper, that is, a mind functioning partially, sometimes or even often functioning irrationally. Significant learning in schools is the learning of academic subjects, sciences and arts, but also learning in relation to real meditative mind awareness. It is not at all what is suggested here, namely engagement in activity related to illusion and the creation of illusions in the mind.

3.40

Brown & Moffett: The hero begins in a state of innocence and unconsciousness and ends in a state of grace and higher consciousness .... The hero is ultimately an earthly manifestation of transcendental and enduring universal principles and patterns in human experience.

Commentator: This statement is made by writers who assume that consciousness is absolute, that all of awareness is consciousness. Profound, meditative mind intelligence, understanding, and wisdom relate to awareness beyond consciousness and not to some partially functioning mind projection called a "state of grace" or "higher consciousness." Any heroine or hero is merely a thought-created, mind-projected "self," hence nothing ultimately real, that is, nothing living, and the so-called "universal principles" spoken about here are equally mere projections out of a partially functioning mind and not what is really the universal, the whole, the all which is the living, what really is, the eternally alive with which there can be communion when there is mind in a truly meditative state. "Patterns ... in experience" are as inert and dead as is all that is experience, and there cannot be anything of the new, the alive, the dynamic and ever-changing in them. Were one to suggest that a teacher and students in a classroom should focus on such patterns so as to understand profoundly, one would be suggesting that they engage in futile, illusion-related activity.

3.41
Brown & Moffett: To take the hero's journey is to expose ourselves to risk and opportunity. It is to open ourselves to the possibilities of hope and despair.
Commentator: Hope and despair are merely opposites, and, so long as one merely walks in the tunnel of opposites, one walks in darkness, not understanding deeply, profoundly. Only when there is a sloughing off of "the hero" by mind in a truly meditative state, a leaving behind of the status of "hero," only when self and all the inane things which self can and does do are ended, does one, that is, does the mind understand profoundly and deeply. When a teacher in a classroom, for example, steps down off the pedestal, as Krishnamurti would have said, so that he or she and the students who are there with her or him together explore matters of right living, of right relating, there is the possibility of all of them having minds which are lovingly intelligent, deeply understanding minds which function partially, but properly, when there is necessity for them to do so but which are otherwise meditative. Then there is concern and an expending of energy related to a way of living which accords with such intelligence and understanding.

3.42
Brown & Moffett: The embodiment of personal insight and wisdom is known as the "philosopher's stone" ... this stone's deeper significance lies in its representation of the unity, wholeness, and integration within human experience that results from engaging in the process of self-inquiry, exploration, and individuation.
Commentator: Real insight and wisdom are neither personal nor impersonal. Rather they are simply there when there is mind in a truly meditative state. So-called personal insight and wisdom relate to a partially functioning mind, perhaps functioning inappropriately, and, since these are of a partially functioning mind, they cannot at all be related to that real unity, wholeness, and integration which are the living, the what *is*, that which is a matter of experiencing moment to moment rather than what is "within human experience," which is related, that is to say, to what is living, dynamic, and ever-changing and not to what is dead, static, and inert. Significant self-inquiry and exploration are inquiry and exploration which exposes the self for what it is, shows that the self is not anything real, shows that any unity or wholeness which it fashions, and integration

which it thinks it can bring about are mere projections from out of itself, hence things merely ideal, things unreal, things imagined or speculated upon, perhaps things wished for or longed for but nonetheless still things unreal for all of that. To base educational endeavours on what is suggested in this statement is to base it on illusion, on falsehood, rather than on real insight into and understanding of things.

3.43

Brown & Moffett: The philosopher's stone embodies the hope that is at the heart of the hero's journey .... At its deepest level, our quest is to become fully self-aware as individuals and as systems.

Commentator: To base anything on hope, which is merely the opposite of despair, is to base it on the partial, the fragmentary. To move merely and always in the hallway of opposites, for example, merely to talk about individuals and systems is ever to move on the level of the superficial and not on the level of the deep, the profound. The fullness spoken of here is not real fullness, and to engage in a search or a quest to become something merely mind projected, a supposedly real self which is said to be fully conscious or completely aware is to engage in futile activity. What can be said about a teacher who would lead students, even if unwittingly, such that they too engage themselves in futile activities, such that they too walk along a path to illusion?

3.44

Brown & Moffett: The heroic educator learn[s] through experience ... insight and understanding are impossible if we limit our learning to the study of someone else's knowledge ... true education is self-education. Although mentors can guide us and colleagues can share what works for them, ultimately we walk the heroic path toward true awareness and insight alone.

Commentator: As regards living, relating, one does not learn through experience(s), by one's partially functioning mind, for example, reflecting on experiences of some kind, one's own or those of others. Rather in these instances one learns, that is, insight and understanding come to the mind, when there is direct observerless, choiceless observation of what *is* now and in the understanding of this what *is* an immediate going beyond it when such going beyond is appropriate, for example, in the case of violence, hatred, and so on. Only such learning is related to one really knowing the self, what it is and what it does, often inappropriately, even harmfully.

As regards learning about right living or right relating there cannot be mentors, leaders, guides, and so on. Rather there must be self-knowing, that is, one's own meditative mind seeing directly what the self is and what it does, and in the seeing and immediate understanding of the confusion and the conflict it creates a true transcendence of, or a going beyond, them. Such self-knowing will not happen, however, when selves, so-called heroes, walk along a path toward the so-called awareness and insight which are merely projections made by the self, merely the thought in which it engages itself. If and when teachers attempt to lead, to guide, to act as mentors for students in order that theirs might be insight and understanding related to right living, their attempts amount to effort to lead students, unwittingly, into illusion.

3.45

Brown & Moffett: Ultimately, the hero's journey results in a more enlightened and holistic self-awareness on the part of the individual hero or heroine.

Commentator: Enlightenment and holism are there only when there is no self. If self-awareness means awareness of what a so-called real self is, and this is often if not always what it is intended to mean, then such awareness is related not to what is real but what is a mere fashioning or creation by a partially but inappropriately functioning mind. A heroine or hero is merely a self, and journeying by any self, hero or heroine or not, is journeying on a path to illusion. Any teacher who sees himself or herself as a hero or heroine and who encourages students to become heroes or heroines is engaged in activity related to the creation of the unreal, hence the false, the illusory, not at all related to what is real communion with what is real.

3.46

Brown & Moffett: Vision building is an expression of hope.

Commentator: Vision building is engaging in activity related to what is unreal, to the merely imagined. What is needed in education as regards understanding of living, of really relating, is not so-called teaching and so-called learning in relationship to what is the merely imagined, wished for, longed for, hoped for. What is needed is education related to properly partially functioning minds, to the development of minds which can deal with temporal matters by proper partial mind functioning rather than, when the matter is that of right living, partial functioning of the mind related to projection of visions and the expression of hope rather than despair. What is also needed, however, are totally functioning minds, minds which are meditative, hence open to understanding the psychological aspects of living, matters which have to do with right living, right relationships.

3.47
Brown & Moffett: Heroic educators need personal mastery and emotional intelligence to be able to achieve their vision.
Commentator: Personal mastery implies person or self, a partially functioning mind controlling thoughts, desires, and so on. When there is true meditative mind awareness, however, one asks who is the controller who seeks control, and one sees that the controller is nothing more or nothing other than the controlled. Such seeing allows for the understanding that person or self is ultimately or actually unreal, and so any so-called personal mastery, as well as any so-called emotional intelligence are mere fashionings by an inappropriately partially functioning mind, as unreal as any vision which is fashioned by such a functioning mind. So-called heroic educators who indulge in the illusions voiced here and who strive, even if unwittingly, to initiate students into the entertainment of such or similar illusions are engaged in processes which are the very antithesis, so to speak, of what is right education.

3.48
Brown & Moffett: There is great power in our ability to engage in collaborative dialogue using story, metaphor, and "wisdom tales" from our shared experience .... The journey ... involves a search for wisdom figures – individuals and groups who embody expert knowledge, insight, and truth.
Commentator: Experience is the old, the dead and gone, and the stories which express experience(s) are the result of movement of merely partially functioning minds engaging in activity in the house of the dead. Thus, in spite of what is suggested here, a focusing on experience, on things said, tales told by supposedly wise and so-called experienced people, so-called living or dead, will not, indeed cannot lead to insight into matters related to right living, right relating, and to truth about them. The tales told by these so-called wise ones contain, very often, neither knowledge nor meditative mind insights but rather mere beliefs, opinions, impressions, perhaps illusions, biases, prejudices. Rather than expending energy in the way suggested here, educators could use such wasted energy to explore with colleagues and students meditative mind awareness and matters which have to do with it.

3.49
Brown & Moffett: Organizations are living systems; therefore, the members of a school system must understand the critical role of information flow and feedback loops in shaping and defining their operations.

Commentator: To say that organizations are living is to confuse partially functioning minds and creations of it, like organizations, with fully functioning minds. "Information flow," "feedback loops," and "operations" all relate to mere partial functioning of the mind and hence have nothing to do with the living, the eternally alive, that with which there can be communion in the state of the meditative mind. Only when educators understand and value such a state of mind and the things it makes possible is there the possibility of real revolution in education, something other than the fragmentation that is everywhere there in education today.

3.50

Brown & Moffett: Effective problem solving and change management within the heroic system involve collaboration, vision, and transforming the organizational culture.

Commentator: Vision relates not to what *is* but rather to what is merely imagined or speculated upon. Fundamental change is there when there is choiceless, observerless observation and the insight and understanding which such observation makes possible, rather than partial functioning mind escape into imagination, into illusion. For real transformation in education, there must be no "collaboration" of heroes and heroines, that is, minds which always and only function partially to solve problems of living, of relating, not merely change from one pattern of organization or management to another, but rather concern for and a cultivation in schools of meditative mind awareness, awareness which does not cancel out a need for proper partial functioning of the mind, but which does see the limits of all such functioning, and thus makes possible a real transcendence of such functioning so that there is deep understanding and action related to it.

3.51

Brown & Moffett: In an effective heroic system, information management is a critical part of dealing effectively with conflict, problems, and crisis.

Commentator: Conflict, problems, and crises in living, in relating, are created by partially functioning minds and cannot be solved by a partially functioning mind. Hence, even the best management of information is, and must be, ineffective in dealing with them. In face of such problems, however, there can be choiceless, observerless observation, and out of such meditative mind related observation can come the insight and understanding which are the dissipation of conflict, problems, and crises in living, in relating. What is needed in education, but seldom if ever talked about, is such meditative mind awareness rather than only and always awareness of a partially functioning mind.

3.52

Brown & Moffett: Transformed educators, schools, and systems ... know that their strength comes from relationships .... Because heroic educators know that they can learn from everyone and everything, they open the doors to their schools and invite the community in.

Commentator: Relationships are indeed important for living is relating and really relating is really living. What is needed for right living, right relating, however, is meditative mind awareness and learning related to such awareness. When there is such awareness, relationships can be real rather than merely image ones, ones which involve self, something ultimately unreal, something not living, not related to the eternal, reaching out to another self or to other selves, equally unreal. Profound learning from everyone and everything, however, is not learning on the part of a partially functioning mind but rather is learning from out of a totally functioning one. Any heroine or hero is one whose mind is functioning partially for the heroine or hero is self, that is, a partially functioning mind. Self being there militates against depth of learning from everyone and everything. Such depth of learning, which, if of concern to educators, makes for education revolutionized, is not that which is being spoken about here.

3.53

Brown & Moffett: Transformed educators, schools, and systems know that learning is their lifeblood.

Commentator: Learning is indeed what education is all about. Learning, however, it can be said, is of two types, related to partial functioning of the mind and related to meditative mind awareness. Though there is need, in many schools, for transformation so that there is better learning of sciences and the arts, and perhaps a need also for better standards, evaluation, and so on, in a mind in a truly meditative state there is also the understanding of the need for schools related to the cultivation of minds revolutionized, minds fully and not merely partially educated.

To conclude this chapter, we turn now to a number of statements by Krishnamurti. These statements, like the ones quoted to this point in this chapter, are about educational change. Since, however, these relate to a truly meditative mind, were spoken out of meditative mind awareness, rather than out of awareness which is consciousness and a partially functioning mind, they relate to revolutionary educational change and not to change which can at best be merely reformatory, hence ultimately superficial.

3.54
Krishnamurti: A school means leisure in which to learn. So, [then, are teachers and students] learning, about authority, [violence, jealousy, envy, and so on], tearing [them] to pieces and seeing the facts of [them]?
Commentator: Though in schools there is, and must be, much learning related to partial functioning of the mind, that is, learning science, mathematics, one or several of the arts, there can also be the kind of learning talked about here, learning related to meditative mind awareness, learning related to profound insight and understanding of living and matters related to living. Such learning has to do with observerless and choiceless seeing of what *is*, for example, authority, exercise of power, jealousy, and so on, and with the understanding which comes of such seeing a going beyond such things, real freedom beyond them.

3.55
Krishnamurti: [In schools and universities, teachers and students could] together create a flame of learning.
Commentator: There is a difference between living and thought, but there can be learning in relationship to living and in relationship to thought. Education related to understanding of the whole, the living, and of the parts, that is, academic subjects, the sciences and the arts, has to do with both living and thought, with both thought-related investigation and meditative mind-related investigation. Such education can be there when there is understanding of the difference between conscious awareness and awareness which is not consciousness and the difference between a partially and a fully functioning mind, but also an understanding of the importance of both levels of awareness and functioning, the relative, time-related, and superficial level and the profound, eternity-related one.

3.56
Krishnamurti: [Teachers in educational institutions could] create a different thing altogether ... a different place where all [in them] are learning. And a student coming into the middle of this, what a tremendous thing he [or she would] find: that [people there] really mean what [they] say, that [they] are really learning. I think that is the root of this [matter of education], that [people] are [in schools and universities] to learn from each other, from the books, from the students, and from everything.
Commentator: The learning in this "different place" is learning in a totally revolutionized educational institution, a school, college, or

university which cultivates not only partially functioning minds in relation to knowledge and understanding of academic disciplines, arts and sciences, but which also cultivates fully functioning, truly meditative minds. In this institution, different from most if not all of those which exist at the present time and in which there is merely concern for, and better or worse actual development of partially functioning minds, there is concern for matters related to loving, and not just rational, thought-related intelligence, to right living, right relating, insight and understanding of the eternal and not just the temporal, understanding which, unlike the partial understandings which are possible when the mind functions partially, fragmentarily, is profound.

3.57

Krishnamurti: Apart from mathematics and all the rest of it, [meditative mind learning is the school's] responsibility too, a much greater one .... If [there is not such learning, then] the academic subjects become all important, and then [people within the school, or university walls] are lost.

Commentator: When there is action in any school or university related to the responsibility spoken about here, then this school or university is one which is revolutionized. When there is an exercise of this responsibility, so to speak, on the part of all within it such that teachers and students are really learning about right living, right relating, about meditative mind awareness and what it makes possible, then, though there is proper focus on the development of students' understanding of academic subjects, there is cultivation of the totality of the mind, of the mind which can function partially, but which can also be silent and in its silence in communion with the living, the eternal, the deep, the profound. Those in a school or university whose minds are in such a state of silent communion are not at all lost. Their minds, when in the state of meditative mind awareness, are not only exploring but also discovering what it means to love, to relate rightly with others, with the world.

3.58

Krishnamurti: [If all the teachers in a school or university] plant the seed ... it will operate. [Indeed], the seed will operate right through [the teachers' and students' lives]; *that* will flower.

Commentator: It can be said that what can flower if teachers, when "off the pedestal," plant the seed, that is, explore together with students the nature of the truly meditative mind and matters related to it, is total functioning of the learners' minds, his or her own and that of the students in the classroom with her or him. If and when such flowering occurs or happens as a result of such exploration and discovery in a classroom, then there is education radically transformed, education revolutionized rather than merely reformed.

3.59

Krishnamurti: [As it is now, schools and universities only] awaken ... intelligence to a certain point ... but ... do not make it flower.

Commentator: Full flowering of intelligence means not only the development of a properly partially functioning mind but also the blossoming of loving intelligence in the state of the truly meditative mind. Only schools and universities with a concern for and that expend energy as regards such development and such blossoming are schools and universities really revolutionized.

What we see now in education and in writing about it is most often if not always the fragmentary, the partial, the limited, even the false, the illusory. What is needed in education and everywhere else today is not just minds which function properly but partially, but also minds which function fully, minds which are truly meditative and which make possible things which a merely partially functioning mind might think are impossible.

In the next and last chapter of this book, after a description of a suggested "curriculum" which relates to proper cultivation in universities of the fully functioning mind, an attempt is made to describe the mind of one who is fully educated, one whose mind has flowered or blossomed completely, one who is the "product" of a school or a university which educates not only for proper partial functioning of the mind but also for true meditative mind awareness.

Chapter Four

The Fully Educated Mind

Right education is surely finding a different way of life, setting the mind free from its own conditioning. And perhaps then there can be love, which in its action will bring about true relationship between man and man.

Without goodness and love, you are not rightly educated.

J. Krishnamurti

Indications have already been presented relative to the question of how to cultivate fully functioning, truly meditative minds. What was said by way of proper procedure in this regard would be appropriate at all levels of formal education – elementary, high school, and university. At a university level, however, if philosophy were revolutionized along the lines suggested in *Beyond Metaphysics Revisited*,[1] then philosophy courses which deal specifically with the meditative mind could be part of a student's overall program and could help provide, so to speak, a kind of arch or umbrella of fullness of meaning and purpose which is not there in higher education today.

Such an arch or umbrella would be quite different from that which was there in medieval universities and is there in schools today where religious faith is the basis of what goes on in the classroom. However, just as theology in the Middle Ages was a unifying principle in universities of the day, so now the meditative mind could give holism of sense and purpose in educational institutions. There would be, however, a fundamental difference for theology is of a merely partially functioning mind, and its relationship is to mere mind projections of the timeless and not to the timeless as it really is. Indeed, these projections, that is, dogmas, doctrines, speculations, and imaginings relate not to the real but to the unreal. The transcendence theology suggests is possible is illusory, unlike that which is possible when there is a truly meditative rather than a partially functioning mind.

The arch or umbrella which the truly meditative mind makes possible and which could be there in education today is also, however, quite different from the kind that Ken Wilber calls for when he voices his preference for more right and less left-brain thinking, or rather his desire for an amalgam of both of these types of partial mind functioning, namely vision-logic and the so-called higher levels of consciousness beyond vision-logic which are said to be possible with proper evolution and development of consciousness, and which he suggests can provide holism as regards meaning and purpose in living. His suggestions in this regard relate merely to partial functioning of the mind, but what is of the partial and fragmentary cannot lead to anything other than the partial, the fragmentary. The real whole which is the living and minds which really commune with it are what can really be the arch or umbrella which makes possible deep meaning and purpose in educational settings and elsewhere, indeed everywhere. In classrooms, this umbrella is there when, as was said earlier, ten or fifteen minutes in any period are there for teachers and students to learn about the truly meditative mind and the things which it makes possible, or when, in the teaching of any subject matter, of any academic discipline in a classroom, there is talk about how the particular subject matter or academic discipline can be seen in its proper light, as limited, that is, and not related to reality, the whole, the living, the unknown.

As it is, there is no overall unity or holism as regards meaning and purpose in universities today. Everything is fragmentary, with professors engrossed in and only teaching their own disciplines, often in isolation from what is going on elsewhere in the university. Even within many university departments people walk only and always in the tunnel of opposites, defending their own particular stance relative to the discipline they practice and teach, opposing whenever they can and feel they must, those who hold to a different stance. In psychology and in education, for example, the so-called humanists oppose the so-called analysts and vice versa. In history there is opposition between those who see history as art and those who see it as science, and in philosophy analysts oppose postmodernists and vice versa, and so on.

University education would be radicalized or revolutionized if changes like the following were made.

1. Not only for those who specialize in philosophy revolutionized, philosophy, that is, which is related both to knowledge and to living wisdom concerns, related to partial and to full functioning of the mind, but also for those in other specialties as well there would be courses, possibly one at the beginning and one at the end of a program, which deal with the whole of the mind. Such courses would relate to the understanding that, though the mind can and must function partially, it can also be absolutely silent, meditative, and, that when it is so, things which are not possible for a partially functioning mind are seen to be possible for one which is silent, meditative. In such courses there would be learning both in relation to the partially functioning mind and to the mind which functions totally.

2. The overall university curriculum would be organized into the following broad areas: philosophy (but revolutionized as indicated above), mathematics, the sciences, the arts, and history. There would be no sociology, psychology, and religious departments, or at least not as they currently exist, with their concern only for either right-brain or left-brain partial functioning of the mind. In the history area courses could be offered in which the history of psychology, sociology, and religion would be taught, but no attempts would be made unduly to condition the minds of students with the suggestion that these are anything more than mere creations of partially functioning minds. Should it be decided that psychology and sociology should continue as university departments, they would do so under the arch or umbrella, and they would be revolutionized because they would be based on the realization and the understanding that there is no living self, on the understanding that conscious awareness is not all of awareness, and the understanding that besides a partially functioning mind there can be a completely silent, truly meditative mind. All of these understandings are not there in any of today's organized religions, nor in much if not all of psychology and sociology, particularly, for example, in so-called humanistic, transpersonal psychology. Organized religions, psychology, and sociology must rightly be seen for what they can rightly or wrongly do and what they cannot do. Specialized schools related to practical know-how would continue to operate, but even in these schools teachers would make sure that there is right understanding of what is done in them, understanding that what is done in them is limited and

not the whole, that there is understanding that its programs relate to parts and not to the whole, but also awareness of what is beyond the parts, the limits, and the significance of living in accord with such awareness.

To conclude this chapter and this book, as was said earlier, there follows now a description of a fully educated mind. If the suggested changes in education just outlined, and perhaps others also, were to be made, what kind of minds would there be, or could there be, at the end of students' formal education? An answer to this question, organized under six descriptive phrases, is what follows now.

Observerless Observation and Listenerless Listening

4.0
Krishnamurti: [One who is fully educated is aware that it is important] to observe ... to see things instantly without a distortion when [there is] the danger of prejudice, [violence, jealousy, hatred, and so on].
Commentator: One who is fully educated is knowledgeable in many different areas, and perhaps an expert in one such area, or even in several areas, but she or he is also one whose mind is in an ever-abiding meditative state even as it functions partially when the matter at hand demands such functioning. In the case of such an individual, his or hers is the kind of observation which is necessary in relation to the development and partial mind understanding of knowledge and properly knowledge-related matters, but as regards matters of living, as when there is the danger of prejudice, violence, hatred, hers or his is observerless, choiceless observation. It is this kind of observation which relates to depth of insight and understanding of what it means to live and what it means to die, not only physically but psychologically, which relates to living fully, with the peace and joy which are there when the mind is completely ordered, deeply and immeasurably silent, in communion with what *is*, the eternally alive.

4.1
Krishnamurti: [A totally educated person is aware of the value of] seeing [without any] motive [to] go beyond [something] in order to achieve something [else. He or she sees, for example] only violence, not how to be out of it, or go beyond it, suppress it, and all the rest of it. [She or he sees] what is happening in the world, which is violent, which is in

[himself or herself. He or she sees] that, which means [she or he observes] violence without any distortion, which is without motive.

Commentator: Understanding in the case of the totally educated person is deep or profound for it relates not just to a partially functioning mind but to one which is truly meditative. It relates to a mind which realizes that besides the kind of observation which is proper in relation to physical, temporal matters, what is of concern in science, for example, there is observation without motive, as is said here, without self there at all, and thus it is "without any distortion."

4.2

Krishnamurti: [Because his or hers has been and again and again is] the awakening of intelligence and order, [one who is educated fully sees things] very clearly, and [acts] instantly according to that perception. [She or he is aware] that intelligence [is] to see, for example, that one is greedy, or self-centred, or neurotic, or whatever it is; to see it very clearly and end it immediately, in the twinkling of an eye.

Commentator: This statement, it might be said, points to three descriptors of the mind which is fully educated, mind which has learned and is learning, not only in relation to some part of the superficially functioning mind, but in relation to the truly meditative one. In the case of the fully educated mind, there is, first of all, observerless, choiceless observation as regards living or relating matters. Secondly, there is relative to this kind of seeing instant action, that is, the action of loving intelligence, action which is complete in and of itself. This brings us to the third descriptor, namely the ending of the greed, the self-centredness. As soon as there is the loving action of seeing totally something like the greed or self-centredness that one is, there is dissipation or disappearance of this greedy, self-centred, but ultimately unreal self, of self which might be said to be temporarily real but which, in relation to the eternal, must be said to be unreal.

4.3

Krishnamurti: [One who is completely educated is not at all nationalistic. His or her seeing] nationalism ... and instantly being free of that spirit of tribalism [is] intelligence. [She or he is aware of the importance of] seeing the whole danger of it and ending it immediately. Or attachment, depending on another for one's comfort, depending with all the implications involved in it, seeing that very clearly and dropping it, so [that one is] never attached. Which does not mean [that one becomes] callous.

Commentator: This statement indicates that one who is fully educated deals appropriately with problems of living, problems of relating. He or she is able so to deal with such problems because hers or his is the loving intelligence which sees completely, deeply, without self there to skew or to distort the observation. Such intelligence and the understanding related to it are profound, deep, and related to total attention, to great sensitivity.

4.4
Krishnamurti: [As regards living or relating one who is fully educated is aware of the importance or significance of] the observer [being] the observed, [is aware that] an action coming from [observerless] observation ... is not a postponement, [is action] in which there is no time element at all. [He or she is aware that] seeing that [one is] lazy, or jealous, or whatever it is, that [one is] attached to something, to see it very clearly, and all the implications involved in that perception, and [to]end it [is possible].
Commentator: To see that there are matters which are not time-related and cannot be dealt with, so to speak, in the way that one deals with temporal matters is indication that one's mind can be and is truly meditative. One who is fully educated communes with the eternal even as it functions partially in relation to time whenever such functioning is called for or is appropriate. He or she, however, is not the product of schools which operate on the assumption that a left or right-brain partially functioning mind can envision, image, or conceptualize the eternal, or, if she or he is such a product, he or she has negated the falseness of any such assumption.

4.5
Krishnamurti: [If one is totally educated, one looks at violence, jealousy, and so on,] without any emotional exaggeration, or suppression, or rationalization. [One] just [observes] it.
Commentator: This statement makes clear that one who is fully educated understands that, because there is awareness which is not consciousness, awareness without self in any form there being aware, and, because there can be mind really silent and not always and only functioning partially, there are two kinds of observation. What is appropriate as regards living related matters, he or she is aware, is observerless, choiceless observation. When there is such observation of things like violence, jealousy, and the like, then there is appropriate action relative to the conflict and confusion which accompany them.

4.6

Krishnamurti: [Those who are fully educated are] capable of watching. [They] watch everything that is happening, that girl on the bicycle, clouds, trees, everything.

Commentator: Fully educated people engage in partially functioning mind related observation or watching when the matter is time-related but not when the matter is living. To watch everything, as is suggested here, there must be not only observer observation when this is appropriate and necessary but also observation out of a truly silent mind when the matter is living rather than merely thought related.

4.7

Krishnamurti: [Except when there needs to be observer observing and listener listening, one who is totally educated listens listenerlessly] to everything that is happening both outside and inside, and [learns, without] ideation being formed. [Such a one is aware that as regards living or relating there need not be any] time interval between listening and acting, [that interval to which] effort [and] the response of memory, deeply conditioned, [relate. Such a one is aware that all that is needed is] observation, action.

Commentator: One who is fully educated understands, not only that there are two types of observation, two types of listening, observer and observerless, and listener and listenerless respectively, but in the case of each of observing and listening, he or she also understands the difference between the two types. When there is observer observation, this is proper, is appropriate, if the matter is time-related but not if it has to do with right living, right relating. If there is to be insight into and understanding of what relating rightly or fullness of living really is, then there must be the state of the meditative mind, there must be the kind of observerless observation and listenerless listening which are talked about here, namely, not idea or thought related at all, not related to the time interval between the observation or listening and the partially functioning mind activity which might follow upon the observation, the listening, what Krishnamurti here calls "effort" and "the response of memory." What there is rather is the action of love, and, when there is real love, there is movement related to the eternal and not to time, and so it is immediate, instantaneous. All of this relates to the understanding of one who is fully educated.

Habitless Living

4.8

Krishnamurti: [One completely educated is] supremely intelligent, [and so, seeing that conditioning] of the mind ... is enormous habit, [he or she is aware of the importance of breaking] down the habit-forming machinery in a human being.

Commentator: As regards matters psychological, the totally educated person does not strive or does not exert effort to cultivate so-called good habits to counter so-called bad ones. Psychologically, his or her mind is totally unconditioned, and so her or his living is habitless. In this case choiceless, observerless observation is the breaking down of "the habit-forming" which has long been considered to be important as regards what has been called and still is called "character education."

4.9

Krishnamurti: The easiest way of living [is] forming habits and ruts and grooves and living there, [and] postponement becomes the habit to which we are educated. [Since] the brain always repeats ... repeating becomes part of our education. [All of this, one who is completely educated sees and understands. Rather than simply trying to understand why he or she has some particular habit, one such as this sees] intellectually, reasonably, logically, that habit-forming limits the mind, the activity of the brain and all the rest of it, [sees that it] is a very narrowing little affair.

Commentator: A truly revolutionized mind, psychologically speaking, does not form habits. Its living, therefore, is habitless. It lives in relationship to the dynamic, the new, the fresh, namely, what *is*, the eternally alive, the living. It does not live in a house of the dead, that is, in "habits and ruts and grooves." It is already calmly, quietly moving on the ocean of life. It is like a sturdy, well-built craft sailing down the river of life, effortlessly, with ease, not caught on a sandbar, not out of the mainstream flow of the river in what Krishnamurti, speaking figuratively, would say is a stagnant pool.

4.10

Krishnamurti: [A fully educated individual is one who, psychologically speaking, stops habits], so that the mind is very alert all the time. [She or he] understands why he [or she] has formed habits and what that does to the brain – limits it, conditions it, harms it, makes it small, narrow, petty. [He or she understands] what sensitivity is, [how important it is to be] highly sensitive, watchful, alert, watching others, watching himself [or herself, and thus she or he does not form habits].

Commentator: The alertness of the mind of one who is fully educated is of a truly meditative mind. So alert, so attentive is such a mind that seeing out of it is observerless, listening out of it is listenerless. So "highly sensitive, watchful, alert" is such a mind that it makes possible habitless living, living in relation to what is new and dynamic, the real rather than the merely ideal, the imagined, that which is merely speculated upon, wished for and longed for but illusory.

Freedom From all Psychological and Spiritual Authority

4.11
Krishnamurti: [As regards living or relating, one who is totally educated lives] with no authority and ... no violence.

Commentator: The mind of one who is completely educated is totally free. This freedom is not that limited, relative freedom which is talked about when there is a partially functioning mind but rather is absolute, total freedom of the mind, relating as it does, psychologically speaking, to total unconditioning of the mind. This does not mean that such a person does what she or he likes, acting irrationally, violating necessary civil laws, and so on. What it does mean is the negation of all psychological and so-called spiritual authority. What it means is that one does not look to any so-called guide, guru, mentor, or someone else who claims to know or is dubbed as "knowing" what it is to live, to relate rightly. Because of such negation and the freedom which comes when there is such negation, one's way of living can be out of love rather than out of thought, hence completely without violence, ordered, peaceful, joyful, a way of living related to action which is love, which is truth, rather than merely and always related to engagement in partially functioning mind activities.

4.12
Krishnamurti: [One who is fully educated says,] 'No authority,' [and so she or he is] attacking the most fundamental thing ... breaking down everything man has built, basically ... if there is no authority ... no pressure ... no influence, [then there is freedom. When the mind is totally free, it] is never influenced, and therefore in itself it has the seed of flowering. [There can be] learning together to have a brain and a mind that is not a slave to something, a slave to words, a slave to an idea; to nothing, therefore really free. [This is] absolute freedom. [This is being] free of word/thought/image.

Commentator: When this fully educated person says, "no authority," he or she of course means no psychological, spiritual authority. Living without any such authority, hence without any conditioning as regards one's way of living, any undue influence on it, the mind of such a person is absolutely, completely free. Living, then, is expansive, out of love, out of living truth rather than merely out of thought. In such a person the seed has flowered and flowers again and again.

4.13
Krishnamurti: [Those who are educated completely understand that there can be complete freedom beyond] fear, [rather than merely] momentary cessation of fear.
Commentator: To say this is in effect to say that fully educated people are aware that there are two levels of the mind, that whereon there is partial mind functioning and the other whereon there is absolute, total silence of the mind. For such people there is harmony in relation to the whole of the mind, and thus in relation to both levels of the mind, which means there is partial mind functioning whenever this is appropriate and necessary, as, for example, when the concern is something scientific or technological, or something practical, but no such functioning when such functioning is inappropriate, the cause of confusion and conflict. This also means that the minds of these people are completely silent or meditative when there need be no partial functioning of the mind or when silence of the mind rather than partial functioning is appropriate. One example of when silence rather than partial functioning of the mind is what is appropriate is when there is psychological fear, that is, merely mind-created fear which has no basis in fact. To use a partially functioning mind in face of such fear means there can at best be a "momentary cessation of fear." If, rather, there is a truly silent, meditative mind facing this fear, there can be complete freedom beyond it.

4.14
Krishnamurti: [Psychologically speaking, the fully educated individual lives without any] shadow of authority, [and so his or her] mind is really free.
Commentator: 'Authority' in this statement means psychological or so-called spiritual authority. So long as any such authority is there, there cannot be mind totally unconditioned, completely uninfluenced, hence absolutely, "really free." One who is totally educated lives without any such authority, lives with mind totally, utterly unconditioned, uninfluenced, psychologically speaking.

4.15

Krishnamurti: [As regards living or relating, the one who is totally educated never strives to] learn from examples [for she or he understands that, if one makes effort in relation to such so-called learning, one is] caught ... merely imitating, or being stimulated, which is fatal, which is like taking a drug.

Commentator: When there is so-called learning from examples, one's mind is partially functioning. Though imitation or learning from examples has value and is sometimes appropriate on such a level of the mind, as when, for example, one is learning some technique or craft, it has no value at all as regards right living, right relating, as regards matters psychological. Indeed, then it inevitably leads to confusion, to conflict in living, in relating. As regards matters pscyhological, the learning of one who is fully educated is meditative mind and not partially functioning mind related, hence not at all related to imitation, to "being stimulated," to mind conditioning, and so on, but rather to choiceless, observerless observation out of a completely silent mind, out of the understanding which is integral to such a mind.

4.16

Krishnamurti: [One who is fully educated understands the folly of living in accord with psychological and/or spiritual authority, of living with psychological habits of any kind. She or he understands that unless one sees] the total scene [or sees any particular thing] totally, [sees that] there must be no direction, no prejudice, no motive, [one's] way of living [is] most unintelligent.

Commentator: The mind of the totally educated individual is whole, undivided, nonfragmented, perfectly ordered. It functions with partial intelligence when such functioning is appropriate, but otherwise it is silent, meditative. In its meditative state it understands deeply, lives habitlessly, without any psychological, spiritual authority guiding it down a path leading to illusion. Its understanding is measureless, hence without direction, prejudice, motive. Its intelligence is total, deep, profound, loving.

4.17

Krishnamurti: [Completely educated people] break through [and so are not] frightened of the unknown, [not] frightened to let the known go. [They fully live, understanding that] with fear, [they have] no love, [that] as long as [there is] fear, there is no love.

Commentator: The perfectly ordered minds of fully educated people make for right relationship as regards thought and love, as regards the

known and the unknown. This is to say that such a mind sees that love and
the unknown are absolute and eternal whereas thought and the known are
relative and temporal. It sees that love is beyond fear, not opposite to it,
just as the unknown is beyond and not opposite to the known, and that,
when love or communion with the unknown is there, there is no
psychological fear.

4.18

Krishnamurti: [One who is fully educated understands the] difference
between *knowing* what is said about freedom and *having* that freedom,
being free.

Commentator: Being totally free, psychologically speaking, is possible
only when there is a truly meditative mind. Since in the case of the fully
educated individual there is not only and always a partially functioning
mind but also a truly meditative one, his or her mind is really, totally free.
When such an individual speaks to communicate something about this
totally free state of mind to another, she or he is aware and tells the other
to be aware that anything he or she says about total freedom of the mind
is mere description and not at all the described, that the words which
describe are never themselves what is being described.

Full Intelligence, Total Love, and Living in Relationship to Complete Order

4.19

Krishnamurti: [Fully educated people] use the great mechanical,
reasoning part [of the mind] and go beyond it.

Commentator: This does not mean there will be development or
evolution of the first, namely, reasoning, an aspect of a partially
functioning mind, so that it becomes the other, that is, the truly meditative
mind which relates to the unknown, the eternal mystery which is living.
There can be no continuity of the one with the other, but rather there can
only be the other when the first, the partial, is ended. Only when time and
that which, even if properly, relates to time are negated, is there the
timeless and what relates to it. Without this ending there will be
enterprises like those of Stuart Parker, Tobin Hart, and Brown and
Moffett, for example, for greater emphasis on right-brain thinking and less
on left as a way to effect profound transformation, to bring about deep
understanding, and so on. For the timeless to be, hence for real
transformation and depth of understanding to come to the mind, there must
be, not mind movement through time but rather movement beyond it, or,

there must be movement of a partially functioning mind through time so that it might intellectually understand all that it can, but then at that point to be completely silent so as to go beyond time and its partial functioning.

4.20

Krishnamurti: [Fully educated people] have [the] feeling of awakening of ... extraordinary intelligence and order.

Commentator: This is another way of saying that fully educated people are aware that besides partial functioning mind intelligence and the limited, relative time-related order it makes possible, there can be the full, total, complete intelligence of the truly meditative mind in relationship to living and its communion with measureless, unlimited, absolute, eternal order. It is such communion which makes for a mind which is immeasurably, absolutely, eternally ordered.

4.21

Krishnamurti: [Totally educated people are self-knowing. They are] learning about [themselves], or the way [they] think, [their] motives. [For them, when the matter is one related to living], intelligence is perception, and action [with] no ideation.

Commentator: The self-knowing of such people is not what is often called self-knowing and related to belief in a supposed real self. All talk related to such a supposedly real self coming to know what it really is has no relation to truth but rather to illusion. This is because self – so-called lower or so-called higher – is never anything ultimately real but always merely a fashioning out of thought, out of a partially functioning mind. When there is choiceless, observerless observation of what *is*, observation, that is, without any form of the self there at all, and, when there is no belief in a supposed really living self, no talk related to such a belief, then there can be the loving intelligence of the truly meditative mind and the understanding of living which such intelligence makes possible. Love which is the fullness of intelligence and of a level of the mind different from that on which there is ideation is the only action needed for there to be right living, right relating.

4.22

Krishnamurti: [Totally educated people can rightly answer the question], what is the known? [They are aware that] the known is [themselves, that] the known is all the thing which is [the self and all the things this self fashions].

Commentator: Those who are completely educated have a rational understanding of the known which is time-related. Theirs is, for example, an understanding of science, and theirs is knowledge as related to practical know-how. As regards matters psychological, however, theirs is the self-knowing which is described in this statement, a knowing of the self, what it is and what it does, and also that it is not anything real but rather and always a mere creation or fashioning of a partially functioning mind.

4.23
Krishnamurti: [Completely educated people are] highly intelligent. [They are aware that deep] intelligence is perception and instant action, [and they understand] the dangers of human ignorance. [Their] intelligence [shows them] what is dangerous, and [they] act. [Because their] intelligence [is awakened,] they [are] free.
Commentator: The intelligence of completely educated people is not merely rational, but deeply loving. Their perception is not only and always with perceiver there, but when appropriate, as regards matters of living, of relating rightly, it is perceiverless. Because such people are not only and always engaged in activity of some kind, they act out of love rather than out of thought when the matter at hand is living, is relating rightly.

4.24
Krishnamurti: [In the one who is totally educated there is] the flowering of intelligence.
Commentator: This flowering of intelligence is not only partially functioning mind related but also meditative mind related. Full flowering of intelligence is there only when, besides awareness which is conscious awareness, a partially functioning mind, and the appropriate images and symbols, ideas and concepts which such a mind creates, there is awareness which is not consciousness, a fully functioning, truly silent mind, and the insight and understanding related to it. Only when there is full flowering of intelligence as related to a truly meditative mind can there be living which is holistic and completely filled with meaning rather than fragmented and lacking as regards ultimate meaning, can there be a mind completely unconditioned, hence really free and totally loving.

4.25
Krishnamurti: [Because the individual who is fully educated lives in relationship to the timeless, he or she is] free of ... violence.
Commentator: To live completely or holistically is to live without violence, without any divisiveness or psychological conflict. Such living implies meditative mind awareness, and, when there is such awareness, there is communion not only with the relative, the temporal, but with what

is deep or profound, that is, the absolute, the eternal, in a word, the timeless. Such living is possible when one is fully educated.

4.26
Krishnamurti: [The one who is completely educated is] extraordinarily intelligent, [and] that intelligence will then operate wherever [she or he is. He or she sees] clearly, what [he or she is], what the world is, that the world is [he or she].

Commentator: Extraordinary intelligence is the loving intelligence of a truly meditative mind. Such intelligence can be there when one is fully educated. It can be there, too, even when one's mind must function partially. It is loving, deep intelligence, intelligence related to a truly meditative state of mind which is there when there is that clarity of observerless, choiceless observation which is self-knowledge or self-knowing, that is, seeing what the self is and what it does, that it is not real but that sometimes, though not always, it is appropriate that it be there, that is, when there must be partial functioning of the mind but not when the matter is right living, right relating. When self is not there, there is seeing which is not seeing in relationship to opposites, for example, a partially knowing self or subject facing what it knows as some objective aspect of the physical world. When the matter is living-related, then the seeing is proper only if it is without see-er there, when it it observerless.

4.27
Krishnamurti: [In the case of totally educated people] order and ... intelligence [work] together harmoniously in their lives.

Commentator: Order on the level of the truly meditative mind is complete, as is the intelligence of such a mind. If there is such order, there is this intelligence, and, when this intelligence is there, the mind is perfectly ordered, in communion with the living, completely silent except when it must function partially. Such a mind is that of one who is fully educated.

4.28
Krishnamurti: [One who is fully educated is] totally different from the ... human monsters that are growing up in the world. [It is] because we have no love [that] everything becomes intellectual and verbal, and, therefore, it really has no deep effect.

Commentator: As regards education, this means that, when there is a fully educated mind, there is the fully integrated mind, different from a mind which only and always functions partially, which is never absolutely quiet and so never able to commune with what *is*, the living. The intelligence of such a mind is loving and not merely rational, and, though it makes a place for the properly intellectual and verbal, in its depths it is aware of what is totally beyond, is truly transcendent to intellect and to all that intellect fashions, to all of intellect's ideas, concepts, and theories. It is truly beyond, also, everything which a partially functioning mind might imagine or speculate upon.

4.29

Krishnamurti: [One who is completely educated is aware that real love] cannot be cultivated. [She or he is aware that] it is not a thing that [one individual] can give to [another. The fully educated individual is aware that real love] has nothing to do with sentiment, emotion, romanticism, [that] affection, friendliness, kindness, gentleness, has nothing to do with love. [Indeed, he is aware that love] is a negation of all this, [and that only when there is such negation is there] the other. [This means that] if you have love, all the other things come, but if you [merely] have all these things, as a kind of basketful, the other thing will not happen.

Commentator: A fully educated mind is one which rightly sees possibilities and impossibilities. It sees what is possible and what is impossible as regards a partially functioning mind, sees, that is, that such a mind can function irrationally or rationally. It sees that a rationally functioning mind can rightly, appropriately, successfully deal with the physical or the temporal but not with the living, the eternal. It sees that this impossibility as regards a partially functioning mind is a possibility for a mind which is truly meditative, and this when there is the loving intelligence of such a mind negating all those things which prevent communion with the living, the eternal, the mystery which is the unknown. The truly educated mind sees real differences, for example, the difference between real love and mere sentiment or emotion, between real love which is without self and hence meditative mind and not partially functioning mind related and the affection and friendliness which one person, that is, one self, one partially functioning mind shows towards another person, self, partially functioning mind, or shows towards other persons, selves, partially functioning minds.

Right Relationship, Right Behaviour, and Selfless Living

4.30

Krishnamurti: [Even though she or he sees that] none of us wants to end anything, we just want to carry on for the rest of our lives, [one who is completely educated is one who totally understands the importance of completely ending violence, hatred, and so on].

Commentator: One who is fully educated understands totally, on the level of the truly meditative mind, and it is this seeing which makes for instant action relative to violence, hatred, and so on. It is not seeing on the level of a partially functioning mind involving a time interval between the observation of, for example, violence or hatred, and some so-called action which is a response from memory and which one hopes will eradicate eventually, at some point in time, the violence, the hatred. When an individual who is fully educated acts in relationship to living, his or her action is the action of love, is action in relation to living truth. This makes the action real since it is nor mere engagement in partially functioning mind activity which one wrongly thinks can and will enable one to deal successfully with living-related matters and so bring some measure of peace and order to one's living.

4.31

Krishnamurti: [One who is completely educated is] totally out of the world ... because the world is full of self-interest. [His or her being] out of the world ... implies [that she or he] no longer belong[s] to the world which is full of self-interest, full of status, position, prestige, platforms, and motives.

Commentator: The mind of one who is totally educated is truly meditative, functioning partially only when it must. When there is the truly meditative mind and no partial functioning of the mind at all because there is no need for it so to function, self is not there. All of this means that, though one is always physically in the world, psychologically one does not live in accord with the false values of the world, one does not participate in its futile activities, does not indulge in all of its illusions. Such a one is quite different, however, from hermits, monks, yogis, zen masters, and the like, that is, those who, though they are not in the world since they have left the world to live apart from it, for example in an ashram or a monastery, nevertheless share the same basic values as those who are still in it. Simply to call their values "spiritual" rather than "material" does not mean they are fundamentally different from those of people who choose not to live physically apart from the world. Only eternal values are fundamentally different from merely sensate ones.

All those people who choose to live physically apart from the world have minds which are only and always partially functioning. As their minds function partially, they imagine they are communing with the eternal, but that with which they are communing is merely some projection from out of their partially functioning minds. Their "not being in the world" means they have escaped from the world into a mind created world of illusion, but all the while they think that, since they are not physically "in the world" because they are isolated from it, they are in communion with the real, the living, the eternal. Their partially functioning minds have carried over into their preserved "worldliness" their own false worldly values, and so, as much as the ambitious, self-concerned businessman, they too are ambitious as regards so-called growth and advancement of their so-called spirits, souls, inner selves which are merely partially functioning mind created. Their efforts to get or to acquire virtue and then to act virtuously in so-called service and the doing of charitable deeds are not fundamentally different from the self-interests and the getting and spending which are there in today's financial and business world. How different from these is he or she who is in the world, that is, has not physically escaped from the world but nevertheless is not of the world, who lives "out of the world," that is, not in relation to false, worldly values but rather in relation to the eternal ones – real love, profound joy, peace which the world as it is cannot give, order which is complete and without limits, hence which is immeasurable.

4.32

Krishnamurti: [The individual who is wholly educated is aware that, when and] because [she or he is] confused, [he or she is] the world, [is] what the world is, that terrorist, the divisions ... the whole business. [Because of this awareness, the fully educated individual is not] trapped in that individuality that [she or he is] totally separate from everybody else [and so it is necessary to] battle [in order] to establish [her or his] relationship with the rest of the world. [Rather, he or she is aware] that [she or he is] the world. [His or hers is a complete understanding of] the whole significance of feeling separate, [and thus she or he is really beyond] all the national, geographical, religious, psychological separations.

Commentator: To have a mind beyond all divisions, all separations, is to have a mind totally unconditioned, totally uninfluenced, a mind which does not look to any so-called psychological or spiritual authority to lead or guide it. Such a mind is that of one who is fully educated. When so educated, one's mind looks, choicelessly and observerlessly at what *is*, and its selfless, direct looking at what *is*, the living, means there can be understanding of it. This understanding is what makes for loving intelligence, insight into what is right living, right relating.

4.33
Krishnamurti: [Though the one who is fully educated is in] a rotten society, a rotten world, [he or she is not of it. He or she choicelessly, observerlessly observes] the whole world of relationship with everything, [fully understands it and lives rightly in relationship to it. When this fully educated individual sees] something dangerous, [she or he] never touch[es] it. [Hers or his is] instant action, that is transformation.
Commentator: Because ours is a rotten society, one which is based on political, religious, and other divisions and separations, a person who is completely educated is one whose mind is not always and merely partially functioning but rather is profoundly silent or meditative when there is no need for such functioning. She or he is not of this society, of this world. Though in the world, she or he is not of it, and, because he or she is not, his or her mind is one which is truly transformed, really revolutionized.

4.34
Krishnamurti: [One who is totally educated never enters] into that game [which has to do with the suggestion that stripping away the ego will lead to discovery of a so-called real, true self. He or she understands that this] game that [people] have played umpteen years, or a million years, about the 'real self' ... is bunk.
Commentator: It is precisely this game which is being played by many academics in psychology and religion, like Ken Wilber, Anthony De Mello, and Deepak Chopra, but also, as we have seen earlier in this book, by Stuart Parker, Tobin Hart, and Moffett and Brown, for example, in the area of education. When there is the truly meditative mind, that mind which is seen as having absolute value by one who is fully educated, there is depth of understanding, which means there is loving and not merely rational intelligence. One who is truly intelligent sees illusion or falsehood for what it is. One example of what it sees as false, as illusion, is belief in self as something ultimately real.

Transformation

4.35
Krishnamurti: [One who is fully educated sees and deeply understands the importance of living with] no motive ... no self-interest. [He or she likewise understands the] basic necessity of transformation, [that is], radical transformation of the human mind.
Commentator: This is not transformation as we see it talked about, for example, in Tobin Hart. When there is only and always a merely partially

functioning mind, as in the case of Tobin Hart, there can only be the superficial, for example change which is mere reformation and not change which is revolutionary. When one is fully educated, intelligence in her or his case has flowered and continues flowering completely This is to say his or her mind can properly but also appropriately function partially when necessary, but it can also be absolutely silent, in deep, loving communion with what *is*, the living.

4.36

Krishnamurti: [The one who is totally educated understands that, on the level of the psychological], radical change in the human mind ... implies no conforming, not conforming to a pattern ... to any authority, the authority of [one's] own experience, or the authority of another. [He or she understands that] radical change is eliminating time altogether, not saying I will be something, I will change, later on.

Commentator: This statement indicates in part, that, when there is a fully educated mind, there is a valuing, not merely of a properly but partially functioning mind, hence a valuing of time and time-related matters, but a valuing also of the completely functioning, truly meditative one and of things properly related to it. When there is the truly meditative mind, there can be living in communion with the living, the ever new and dynamic rather than a way of living merely associated with a partially functioning mind, a mind which might foolishly follow some pattern or authority with the hope that deep meaning in living will be the result of its following, its being led down a path to illusion. When there is always and only a partially functioning mind, one always and only lives out of a part or a fragment of the mind rather than out of the eternally present moment, out of a state of mind wherein there is communion with the eternally present moment.

4.37

Krishnamurti: [Anyone who is fully educated sees the importance of] radical, deep, psychological change, [the need for a person to be] totally different, not a superior entity, just ... different, [to] have love.

Commentator: A truly, completely educated mind sees the difference between thought and love, sees that each is related, not to the other, but to a different level of the mind, thought to that of partial functioning and love to that of full functioning. When there is such a mind, there is awareness of where thought is proper, as, for example, in the pursuit of scientific knowledge, and where it is not, namely, when the concern or the matter is right living, right relating. When there is thought, there is self, and, where there is self, there is not and cannot be real love. This is clear to a mind in a truly medititative state.

4.38

Krishnamurti: [The entirely educated person lives out of that] part of the brain which is untouched, unconditioned.

Commentator: A partially functioning mind is always a conditioned mind. One who is truly educated understands that sometimes conditioning of the mind is proper, for example when the matter is something technical, something which is skill-related. Such a one also understands, however, that often conditioning of the mind is the cause of conflict and confusion, of living in relation, not to truth or to what *is*, but rather in relation to what is false or illusory, something merely mind-projected, merely imagined, merely something for which one wishes. Such understanding which is there when there is negating of the false or the illusory is in and of itself unconditioning of the mind, and it makes possible, therefore, complete freedom of the uncontaminated mind. When a mind is totally, utterly free, then it is untouched or uncontaminated, hence pristine, in real communion with what *is*, the living, the absolute, the immeasurable.

4.39

Krishnamurti: [Fully educated people] go into [themselves to] see exactly where [they] are; whether [they] are superficial ... half-way serious ... half-way deep, or really concerned profoundly. [They understand] why mediocrity is always superficial.

Commentator: The minds of those who are completely educated are profound or deep rather than superficial. Such minds function superficially and partially when such functioning is necessary but not when it can be the cause of confusion and conflict. When not functioning partially, truly meditative minds, minds which are totally educated, are deeply silent, higly alert and sensitive, in communion with the living, the immeasurable, the absolute, the mystery which is unknowable.

4.40

Krishnamurti: [Totally educated people] behave with superexcellence [in] their lives [for each of them is] a different human being.

Commentator: Excellence as related to proper partial mind functioning is there when mind is totally educated. Also, however, there is superexcellence as regards the right behaviour which is right living, right relating. Total excellence is there if, in addition to proper partial mind functioning, there is always also real silence of the mind, in the background so to speak when the mind is functioning partially, but completely, absolutely, in the foreground and in the background when there need be no such functioning at all. When there is proper rational, but never irrational partial mind functioning, when there is, this is to say, excellence as regards partial functioning of the mind, but also the superexcellence of mind in a truly meditative state, then there is the fully living human being, quite different from many if not most of the so-called humanly living beings in the world today. Fullness of education relates to minds which are not only excellent but also superexcellent, so to speak.

4.41

Krishnamurti: [Because, in relationship to living or relating, theirs is] intelligence, perception, and action, [fully educated people are] free of jealousy, [anger, hate, violence, and so on] completely, totally and forever, not occasionally.

Commentator: When there is the state of the truly meditative mind, intelligence is supreme, perception is perceiverless, and action is instantaneous. Such intelligence is loving, and a truly loving mind is a mind totally free, completely unconditioned, psychologically speaking. It functions partially when such functioning is appropriate, but otherwise it is absolutely quiet, in communion with what *is*, the living. Such a mind is the mind of those who are totally educated.

4.42

Krishnamurti: [Since deep] intelligence [is] perception and action instantly, [the completely educated person understands that whenever the matter is living or relating, then] perceiving is acting [rather than there being] perception, a long interval, then acting. [Such a person is aware that as regards living or relating] perception does not take place if there is the observer and the observed, if there is prejudice, if the past controls the attitude or the activity in the present. [She or he is aware that] freedom from all that is to observe without prejudice, [and] in that very observation is action ... the ending of something, [for example, the ending of] jealousy completely ... so that [one is] never jealous again.

Commentator: Perception which is immediate action is of a truly meditative mind whereas when there is an interval between perception and ensuing activity of some kind there is perception as related to a partially functioning mind. The perception of those whose minds are completely educated is both with perceiver there and perceiverless, depending upon whether the matter at hand is thought or living-related, out of thought or out of love. One's perception is of the observer type when, for example, one's partially functioning mind is engaged in the doing of science or when one is attempting to solve a practical problem. When, however, the matter is psychological, living-related, then one's perception is perceiverless.

4.43
Krishnamurti: [People who are entirely educated] go into [things like violence, jealousy, and so on,] to the very depths, [so that they observerlessly see and completely understand these things. This] seeing ... is intelligence. And intelligence says, 'Wipe [these things] out.'
Commentator: To go to the very depths of anything which is living-related one's mind must be in a truly meditative state, that state of mind which is requisite if there is to be a fully educated mind. In such a state the mind can understand fully, completely. Then its intelligence is loving, and this intelligence acts instantly. Any living-related problem it faces is solved instantly.

4.44
Krishnamurti: [Totally educated people] ask fundamental questions and find an answer for them, not verbally, but in [themselves], deeply.
Commentator: When there is a completely educated mind, there are no on-going psychological problems for the perceiverless perception and loving intelligence of such a mind are the instantaneous solution of any such problem as soon as it arises. Such a solution is a real one, not one which a partially functioning mind thinks is possible when it moves inward, there supposedly to discover and commune with what it thinks is real but which is merely a creation of its own partial functioning, namely, a so-called soul or spirit.

4.45
Krishnamurti: [As regards the psychological, living, one who is completely educated is] really not concerned with ideas, but with action.
Commentator: One who is completely educated is aware that left-brain partial functioning of the mind, that functioning which results in the creation of ideas, concepts, and theories, is not what is appropriate as regards right living, right relating. Such a one is also aware that no right-brain partial functioning which leads to the fashioning of images and symbols has anything to do with such living, such relating. He or she is aware that what is appropriate as regards living or relating is meditative mind awareness.

4.46

Krishnamurti: [One who is fully educated lives] without a motive, [and this] implies enormous inward clarity. [She or he understands that] freedom ... implies a relationship with each other which is non-authoritarian, [but also understands] that having no authority does not imply disorder, having no authority does not imply each one does what he likes. [The totally educated individual's is a] non-authoritarian way of living. [In her or his way of living there is] order without authority.

Commentator: The clarity of mind of one who is completely educated is total for the completely educated mind is aware and clearly understands when partial functioning of the mind is appropriate, but it also is aware when such functioning is not, when, rather than there being partial mind functioning there must be complete silence of the mind. Such awareness is indication of the complete order which is there when there is not only a partially functioning mind but also one which is truly meditative. The mind of one fully educated functions rationally, but partially, when it needs to, but otherwise it is absolutely quiet, in communion with the living, the eternal, the immeasurable, the unknowable.

Such, then, is one description of the fully educated mind. By way of summary, it might be said that any fully educated mind observes obserververlessly and listens listenerlessly, lives habitlessly, psychologically speaking, is free from all psychological and so-called spiritual authority. Such a mind is fully intelligent, totally loving, and lives in complete order. It relates and behaves rightly, and lives selflessly. It is a mind completely transformed, totally revolutionized, radically changed. The time is now for educational change related to the cultivation of not only minds which function partially but properly, but also to the cultivation, so to speak, of minds which are truly meditative.

References

Introduction:
A Call for Revolution in Education

1. J. Richard Wingerter, *Beyond Metaphysics Revisited: Krishnamurti and Western Philosophy* (Lanham, MD: 2002) and *Science, Religion, and the Meditative Mind* (Lanham, MD: 2003).
2. J. Krishnamurti, *Commentaries on Living*, edited by D. Rajagopal (Wheaton, IL: Quest Books, 1967), vol. 2, p. 239.
3. Ibid., vol. 2, p. 90.
4. Ibid., vol. 2, pp. 71, 125.
5. Ibid., vol. 3, p. 8.
6. Ibid., vol. 3, p. 87.

Chapter One: Teaching, Learning, and the Partially Functioning Mind

1. John P. Miller, J.R. Bruce Cassie, and Susan M. Drake, *Holistic Learning: A Teacher's Guide to Integrated Studies* (Toronto: OISE Press, 1990).
2. Stuart Parker, *Reflective Teaching in the Postmodern World: A Manifesto for Education in Postmodernity* (Buckingham, UK and Philadelphia, PA: Open University Press, 1997).
3. Tobin Hart, *From Information to Transformation: Education for the Evolution of Consciousness* (New York: Peter Lang, 2001).

  From Miller, Cassie, and Drake, *Holistic Learning: A Teacher's Guide to Integrated Studies* (Toronto: OISE Press, 1990).

Specific quotes listed by Chapter Section:

1.0	p. 2
1.1	p. 3
1.2	pp. 8-9
1.3	p. 17
1.4	pp. 17 & 39
1.5	pp. 22-23
1.6	p. 24
1.7	p. 27
1.8	p. 32
1.9	pp. 38-39
1.10	p. 65

From Parker, *Reflective Teaching in the Postmodern World: A Manifesto for Education in Postmodernity* (Buckingham, UK and Philadelphia, PA: Open University Press, 1997).

Specific quotes listed by Chapter Section:

1.11	p. 6
1.12	p. 41
1.13	p. 42
1.14	p. 46
1.15	p. 116
1.16	p. 118
1.17	p. 141
1.18	p. 143
1.19	Ibid.
1.20	p. 146
1.21	p. 148
1.22	p. 149
1.23	p. 150
1.24	Ibid.
1.25	pp. 151-152
1.26	p. 152
1.27	p. 157
1.28	p. 159

From Hart, *From Information to Transformation: Education for the Evolution of Consciousness* (New York: Peter Lang, 2001).

Specific quotes listed by Chapter Section:

1.29	p.	1
1.30	p.	6
1.31	Ibid.	
1.32	p.	8
1.33	p.	9
1.34	p.	11
1.35	p.	12
1.36	Ibid.	
1.37	p.	34
1.38	p.	60
1.39	p.	63
1.40	p.	65
1.41	p.	71
1.42	p.	75
1.43	p.	87
1.44	p.	101
1.45	p.	113
1.46	p.	119
1.47	p.	139
1.48	p.	141
1.49	p.	143
1.50	p.	147
1.51	pp.	156-157
1.52	p.	163
1.53	p.	171

Chapter Two: Teaching, Learning, and the Fully Functioning Meditative Mind

1.   J. Krishnamurti, *A Flame of Learning: Krishnamurti with Teachers* (The Hague: Mirananda, 1993).

Specific quotes listed by Chapter Section:

2.0   pp. 137, 94, 25, 19
2.1   pp. 14, 132
2.2   p. 98
2.3   pp. 99-100
2.4   p.   7
2.5   p. 15

2. J. Krishnamurti, *This Light in Oneself: True Meditation* (Boston: Shambhala, 1999), p. 66.

From J. Krishnamurti, *A Flame of Learning: Krishnamurti with Teachers* (The Hague: Mirananda, 1993).

Specific quotes listed by Chapter Section:

2.6   p. 190
2.7   p.   8
2.8   p. 187
2.9   p.   15
2.10   p.   11
2.11   p.   68
2.12   p.   69
2.13   p.   82
2.14   p.   67
2.15   p.   63
2.16   pp. 20-21
2.17   pp. 187-188
2.18   p. 201
2.19   p. 205
2.20   pp. 114-115
2.21   pp. 89, 204
2.22   p. 205
2.23   p. 204
2.24   p. 203
2.25   p. 202
2.26   p.   88
2.27   pp. 120-121
2.28   p. 156

2.29	pp.	33-34
2.30	p.	31
2.31	p.	84
2.32	p.	19
2.33	p.	10

3. Stuart Parker, *Reflective Teaching in the Postmodern World: A Manifesto for Education in Postmodernity* (Buckingham, UK and Philadelphia, PA: Open University Press, 1997).

    Tobin Hart, *From Information to Transformation: Education for the Evolution of Consciousness* (New York: Peter Lang, 2001).

    John L. Brown and Cerylle A. Moffett, *The Hero's Journey: How Educators Can Transform Schools and Improve Learning* (Alexandria, VA: Association for Supervision and Curriculum Development, 1999).

    From J. Krishnamurti, *A Flame of Learning: Krishnamurti with Teachers* (The Hague: Mirananda, 1993).

    Specific quotes listed by Chapter Section:

2.34	p.	12
2.35	Ibid.	
2.36	p.	168
2.37	Ibid.	
2.38	pp.	169-170, 179
2.39	p.	167
2.40	p.	107
2.41	p.	55
2.42	p.	180
2.43	p.	78
2.44	p.	202

Chapter Three:
Schools and the Meditative Mind

1. Maurice R. Berube, *Beyond Modernism and Postmodernism: Essays on the Politics of Culture* (Westport, CT: Bergin & Garvey, 2002).

    Valerie E. Lee and Julia B. Smith, *Restructuring High Schools for Equity and Excellence: What Works* (New York: Teachers College Press, 2001).

    Joseph P. McDonald, *Redesigning School: Lessons for the 21ˢᵗ Century* (San Francisco: Jossey-Bass, 1996).

    Specific quotes listed by Chapter Section:

3.0	Lee & Smith,	p.	4
3.1	McDonald,	p.	21
3.2	Berube,	p.	3
3.3	Berube,	pp.	32-33
3.4	McDonald,	pp.	153 & 159
3.5	Lee & Smith,	p.	153
3.6	McDonald,	p.	248
3.7	Berube,	p.	23

2. Kathleen Sernak, *School Leadership – Balancing Power with Caring*, foreword by Nel Noddings (New York: Teachers College Press, 1998).

    Specific quotes listed by Chapter Section:

3.8	p.	ix
3.9	p.	x
3.10	p.	3
3.11	p.	18
3.12	p.	23
3.13	pp.	25-26
3.14	p.	26
3.15	p.	28
3.16	p.	44

| 3.17 | p. 45 |
| 3.18 | p. 144 |

3. Douglas J. Fiore, *Creating Connections for Better Schools: How Leaders Enhance School Culture* (Larchmont, NY: Eye On Education, 2001).

    Specific quotes listed by Chapter Section:

    | 3.19 | p. xi |
    | 3.20 | Ibid. |
    | 3.21 | Ibid. |
    | 3.22 | p. xii |
    | 3.23 | p. xvi |
    | 3.24 | p. xvii |
    | 3.25 | Ibid. |
    | 3.26 | p. 130 |
    | 3.27 | pp. 130-131 |
    | 3.28 | p. 139 |
    | 3.29 | pp. 141-142 |

4. Andy Hargreaves (ed.), *Rethinking Educational Change with Heart and Mind*, foreword by Frances Faircloth Jones (Alexandria, VA: Association for Supervision and Curriculum Development, 1997).

    Specific quotes listed by Chapter Section:

    | 3.30 | p. v |
    | 3.31 | p. vii |
    | 3.32 | p. ix |
    | 3.33 | Ibid. |
    | 3.34 | Ibid. |
    | 3.35 | pp. xiii-xiv |

5. John L. Brown and Cerylle A. Moffett, *The Hero's Journey: How Educators Can Transform Schools and Improve Learning* (Alexandria, VA: Association for Supervision and Curriculum Development, 1999).

Specific quotes listed by Chapter Section:

3.36	pp. vii-viii
3.37	p. viii
3.38	p. 1
3.39	Ibid.
3.40	p. 12
3.41	p. 18
3.42	p. 20
3.43	pp. 24-25
3.44	p. 28
3.45	p. 53
3.46	p. 85
3.47	p. 86
3.48	pp. 103-104
3.49	p. 115
3.50	p. 140
3.51	p. 141
3.52	p. 154
3.53	p. 155

From J. Krishnamurti, *A Flame of Learning: Krishnamurti with Teachers* (The Hague: Mirananda, 1993).

Specific quotes listed by Chapter Section:

3.54	p. 64
3.55	p. 65
3.56	p. 64
3.57	p. 78
3.58	pp. 148, 62
3.59	p. 161

Chapter Four:
The Fully Educated Mind

1.   J. Richard Wingerter, *Beyond Metaphysics Revisited: Krishnamurti and Western Philosophy* (Lanham, MD: University Press of America, 2002).

From J. Krishnamurti, *A Flame of Learning:
Krishnamurti with Teachers* (The Hague: Mirananda,
1993), listed by Chapter Section:

4.0	p.	89
4.1	p.	86
4.2	p.	101
4.3	pp.	101-102
4.4	p.	138
4.5	p.	139
4.6	pp.	56-57
4.7	pp.	181-183
4.8	p.	51
4.9	pp.	59-60, 175-176
4.10	pp.	53-55
4.11	p.	94
4.12	pp.	61-62, 174
4.13	p.	166
4.14	p.	65
4.15	p.	24
4.16	p.	110
4.17	p.	130
4.18	p.	19
4.19	p.	22
4.20	p.	100
4.21	pp.	184-185
4.22	p.	130
4.23	p.	113
4.24	p.	78
4.25	p.	79
4.26	p.	90
4.27	p.	97
4.28	pp.	196-197
4.29	pp.	199-200
4.30	p.	111
4.31	pp.	37-38
4.32	pp.	70-73
4.33	pp.	74, 76
4.34	p.	149
4.35	pp.	191-192
4.36	p.	195

4.37	p. 202
4.38	p. 105
4.39	p. 136
4.40	pp. 11, 67
4.41	p. 107
4.42	pp. 102-103
4.43	pp. 134-135
4.44	p. 137
4.45	p. 194
4.46	pp. 42-43

Index

ABOUT THE AUTHOR

J. Richard Wingerter is a retired teacher living in Calgary, Alberta, Canada. Prior to his retirement in 1997, he taught school in Saskatchewan and Alberta. In 1973, he authored two articles entitled "Pseudo-Existential Writings in Education" and "Not Who but What is Pseudo?" which were published in *Educational Theory*. His other books, both published by University Press of America, Lanham, Maryland, are *Beyond Metaphysics Revisited: Krishnamurti and Western Philosophy* (2002) and *Science, Religion, and the Meditative Mind* (2003).